MY TALK JANUARY 2021 – BOOK TWO

TABLE OF CONTENTS

1) Thoughts — Pages 2, 8-13, 50 – 51

2) Knowledge — Page 25 – 28, 35 – 40, 48 – 49, 63 – 64

3) Isiah and Isiah Laing Dream — Page 5 – 7

4) Mixed Race Indian Dream — Page 14

5) Warren Buffet Dream — Page 14 – 15

6) Jamaican Dream — Page 15 – 19

7) My Dream — Page 3, 19 – 24, 41, 44 – 47

8) Louis Farrakhan — Page 29 – 32

9) My Spiritual Bath — Page 33 – 35

10) "AND I SEE THE TEARS ON THEIR LIPS" DREAM — Page 41 – 44

11) Russian Fashion Industry Dream — Page 51 – 52

12) Blackman Dream — Page 53 – 59

13) Dwayne the Rock Johnson & Big Show Dream — Page 60

14) Diana Ross And Anita Baker Dream — Page 60 – 61

15) Shaquille O'Neal Dream — Page 61 – 62

16) TAXES DARK BLUE WATER DREAM — Page 65

17) JOE BIDEN – AMERICAN WAR DREAM — Page 65 – 68

 Dreams are my stay in life.
A way into the past.
The here and now.
The future.
What I see, you cannot see.
What I know I have to show you.
Teach you.
How you get it, comprehend me.
My dreams.
My world.
What I am trying to teach you is truly up to you.

For some I am a threat.
Crazy; weird.
Living out there.
Is out there.
See too much.
Don't know what I am talking about.

Some truly don't care.
What I see many truly do not believe.
But not believing is good for me.
Knowledge is key.
Key to the truth of our past, present, and future.

This is my second book of 2021, and I am hoping if you know the people in this book and others, you will warn them, lead them to the truth of what I see that is to come in their life tomorrow. And no, tomorrow is not the next day in many cases.

Tomorrow is a week, two weeks, a month, months, days, years for me. But however you look at it, you are my help and cornerstone to those that I see. Therefore, please do for me and God and tell; warn those that truly need to be warned if you can.

You don't have to like me. But do not be a closed door to me and or, me. Be my open door if you can.

Many things I see.

Some things I cannot explain.

Many things I cannot do thus, I am relying on you to truly help me.

Know; there are places I cannot go into. This is God's way of ensuring my safety.

God truly do not permit any Child of Life to go into dirty and unclean places. Therefore, know how God protects you here on Earth.

There's a lot more to come therefore, stay in the know because your future, and the future of your true loved ones depend on it – you being in the know.

Michelle.

MY TALK JANUARY 2021 – BOOK TWO

Onwards I go because it's January 12, 2021 and my dream world is waking up. Therefore, Lovey please do not let my writing be hard or cumbersome for me. Dreamt pages – <u>lots with writings on them and these pages were heavy.</u> Therefore Lovey, I need you to tremendously lighten my load of writing. Meaning, do not let all that I write go in vain, or be heavy for me in any way.

I need the eyes of all who read these books no matter the colour, creed, gender, race to be opened to the truth of Life – You. I cannot do without you. I have to write what I see. This is what I've been tasked with when it comes to you here on Earth.

Certain places you've forbidden me to go in therefore, I need true helpers here on Earth and in the Spiritual Realm to help me in getting the messages I get via my dream world, waking state visions, and more to those that are written about in this book and others. I cannot do it alone Lovey come on now. I need true help.

<u>Further, I need the truth to be known globally because whether humans care to know. THE WORST IS YET TO COME.</u>

Lovey, I truly need to save those who truly need you.
I need to be truly there for you in a good and true way.

Lovey, I am passionate about what I write because whether you know it or not, you are in the midst of what I write. You of yourself know if I could write beautiful songs of truth and true praise that people listen to and go wow, Michelle wrote that for God I would. Right now; all I have are dreams, visions, you, and more.

The way I feel; if all who read these lines can feel the way I feel when I write for you Lovey then I would be more than honoured. You are my worth, true worth, and praise Lovey come on now. You know this.

Therefore, the books I write must have life, give true life, true worth, healing to those who need healing, truth to those who need truth, and more good and true things.

It's 2021 Lovey and I truly cannot let you go. You know my feel. And I am going to stop because I need you no matter what and you know this.

Therefore, please do not let my writings which is apart of us be burdensome in any way.

True Life
True Healing
True Praise
True Life's Worth
True Love

True Moral Values
True Teachings
True Thoughts
True Goodness of Everything must come out of these books Lovey.

Now with that said about the dream I had with paper and writings on it. Lovey I am pouting given what I wrote about the Bible in <u>**THE NEW BOOK OF KNOWLEDGE BOOK ONE AND TWO.**</u> Do I have to go and read Isiah of man's so-called holy bible?

Lovey I truly do not want to sin in that way.

I don't want to read Isiah Lovey come on now. Can't I be disobedient in this way and bypass reading Isiah?

Yes, I know I have to key to Life and Death. The key has not passed hands yet to the New Successor, but Lovey do I have to read Isiah?

I don't want to sin Lovey come on now.

Oh God Lovey.

ISIAH, AND ISIAH LAING DREAM.

Both are truly nasty.

<u>*As for you Isiah Laing (the Jamaican Promoter) you are being warned.*</u> Your life right now is truly not yours and I so do not want to get into it because you <u>*are a nasty, and evil human being.*</u> But because I see, I have to write.

<u>*Because I see, I know.*</u>

Dreamt not too long ago as it's after 2pm in the afternoon, *<u>Isiah and Isiah Laing.</u>*

There were two white plastic bottles. It looked like parasites – long parasites were in these two (2) plastic bottles. Parasites that looked like the intestines of a human. These long parasites and or, intestines were in blood about halfway in the bottle. <u>*Isiah Laing was the name I received.*</u>

So, I do not know if someone is going to cut your belly out because in one bottle, the parasites and or, intestines were healthy, and the other bottle had unhealthy parasites and or, intestines in it.

I do not know if you are going to get a stomach ailment, but you are disgusting Allelujah. I so don't want to get in the spirit, <u>but you are a filthy and disgusting demon.</u>

You know what Lovey let me leave this demon alone. Let him be his own warning because he is that disgusting life wise, and spirit wise. God, how I need you to surround me when it comes to this disgusting beast living amongst the living to how disgusting this man is.

As for Isiah, I truly do not want or need to read this book.

However this man dies is truly not my concern.
However humans die globally is truly not my concern.

<u>Earth has and have become the Domain of Death.</u>

<u>Humans truly do not know:</u>

The flesh cannot answer for the Crimes - Sins of the Spirit done here on Earth.
The Spirit is the one to answer for your Crimes - Sins done here on Earth.

After the Flesh is gone then comes the judgement of those who have more Sins than Good, those who are Born of Death, those who have made Sacrifices unto Death, those who have Bleached their Skin, and more.

Onwards I go

Lovey, I truly do not want or need to get into the nastiness of this man. Yes, I know I have the key to Life and Death, but it does not make me feel any better.

Lovey, my countenance is so different because music cannot heal me and or, shield me right now to this disgusting being Isiah Laing.

Why did you have to let me go dream about this living breathing demon?

Murda
Murda
Murda

Allelujah
Drear God
Allelujah

Murda

Murda
Murda

Im dutty
Im dutty
Im dutty

Mi caane tek eee Lovey
Im dutty
Im dutty

Oh God im dutty
Im dutty
Im dutty

Mi caane tek eee Lovey
Mi caane tek eee.

Have mercy on me Lovey. He is condemned now his cup is overflowed with sin.

Death own him literally.

Truly have mercy, and let thy will be done as I put the filth of this man back on him. Take it from me and let him be the one to read his fate in the Book of Isiah of man's so called Holy Bible.

I truly need to be around some clean Spiritual People that is there for me in times like this for real.

Oh God, hell is going to come down to Earth literally and humans globally truly do not know this.

I need to go lay down because I am weak right now.

Hell
Hell
Im hell bound literally.

Allelujah

Michelle

I so do not know if I need to set a table Lovey.

Please tell me what I need to do because I know there is so much more terrible things to come.

Many a guh halla.

Bawl, but this is the life humans globally wanted and needed. They were not thinking of life here on Earth or their life in the Spiritual Realm. Thus, after the Spirit shed the flesh comes the judgement for some – many here on Earth.

In all humans have and has done, they did kill themselves globally. Neither you nor I can worry about this Lovey. Our worry is our saved – good and true own here on Earth and in the Spiritual Realm.

Life is a given. It is humans that take Life from self.
It is humans that deceive self and others.

Thus, I cannot worry about the deceived in life. They have no life in many ways due to them.

This darkness in the Sky Lovey.
This darkness all around Lovey.

What am I missing?

That child I wrote about in Book One.

<u>Is he Death in the Sky?</u>

Oh God let me stop because I am writing again and writing about death weakens me. So, I have to leave Death alone because the worst is yet to come globally it seems.

Michelle
January 12, 2021

There is so much I need to tell you, but I do not know how to begin. *There are doors closed to me when it comes to educating you on Princes.* I truly do not know where to begin because what you think you know about Princes is truly not the truth.

I do not know if I can say *Princes came out of an Order,* and I do not know if I want to open the Brass Door of Old when it comes to discussing Princes and how Princes and or Royalty came about. Thus, certain families when it comes to Princes and or, Royalty you need to stay away from.

Their title is based on evil – the devil thus, the *BLOODLINE* of some. Many families did spill blood to get where they are today. And I am so not going to go any further because some things are truly not good for me.

Because the Spiritual Realm of Evil is not closed off to Earth as yet; you as a person and or, Chosen of God have to be careful. Your spirit can get caught up in the Realm of Evil therefore, I have to let certain things go.

I so cannot explain it any better to you.

Listen, *Brass Doors of Olde has a significant meaning.* Yes, for some they look nice, but the secrets behind these doors go further than you think hence Death, Devil Worship, Sacrifices and Rituals, and more.

Oh God let me stop because certain things you are not to know, and my body is prompting me to stop. Certain things do drain your body of its energy.

Michelle
January 13, 2021

It's January 15th, 2021 and I can't wait for January to be over.

Dream world silent but I know <u>*there is another disease out there to come.*</u> In my dream, <u>*it was White People that were affected by this disease.*</u> And as usual, I am so not going to worry about humans globally. Evil is doing their job. It is humans that refuse to see the truth. Thus, those who speak the truth is either murdered, imprisoned – shut up, and shut down.

Lovey and Mother Earth have been quiet in my world, and this is good I guess in some way.

January is dragging along for me and I am not going to lie, but I've been so candid with God with my feelings.

It's like…no it's not it's like. For me, I want and need God to complete me in a different way and I don't think God and or, Lovey can.

My world is too much like a fairy tale of needs with God.

You know you have absolute truth for someone but that person and or, entity do not have absolute truth for you in the way you need them to. This is the way I feel in terms of God and my setbacks; disappointments in life.

Why can't God be the completion of me?
Why can't God complete the Good and True of this Earth?

Why can't Earth be separated so that Good and Evil live separate as in the Spiritual Realm?

Evil requires all to be dirty thus, Earth is laden in Sin.

However, Good requires a clean and truly peaceful and harmonious environment to live in. Unfortunately, with Evil around, Earth is like unto Sodom and Gomorrah of man's so-called Holy Bible.

Thus, I ask; why do we have so many hurdles to jump over before God finally say enough is enough? No more hurdles, no more trials and tribulations, no more hurt and pain when it comes to me, and the Saved of Life. No more unsurety, no more health issues for my people, just good, true, happy, positive, and clean living from now on.

<u>*EQUAL RIGHTS*</u> *– Peter Tosh*

One of the beauties of life is knowing that God is truly there for you and God is truly there for me, but I need God to truly complete me in a different way. Yes, this is a craving for me, but how do we; God and I and or, Me complete each other to make that positive impact and or, positive difference here on Earth for us, and our good and true own?

How do I surpass my limitations with God here on Earth and connect with God so that God hear me right away and help me, truly complete me with him and or, her so that our life is truly rewarding and meaningful here on Earth?

For me, God is my True Purpose. But, I truly do not know if I am God's True Purpose. Maybe it's my doubt creeping in again, but why would God not complete us in a good, true, positive, clean, truly uplifting, truly happy, truly peaceful, and truly rewarding way?

I truly need a lifestyle change health wise, financially, home wise, Lovey wise, and more. This year and beyond I truly need God to be all that I need God to be and more. I need things to be more than super doper easy in my life for 2021 and beyond and in all I need, do, and want, I need God to be in the midst of it all. I truly do not want or need to go it alone in anything anymore.

I don't know. Maybe I put too much pressure on God.

Maybe I put too much of my all in God, but I truly do not think I put too much of my all in God. If I didn't put all of my all in God, then my life would not have true meaning or purpose.

You know when you are looking for someone or something to give their all as you have done them in life.

That true and more than unconditional love of more than truth that you need and want and put in God. I don't know maybe I want God to live in my fairy tale world with me. It is so different when you see and know what you want and need, and God cannot see it your way or help you your way.

No, I am not in crisis mode.

I am hungry and this is because I've not had breakfast yet and it's 10:57am.

What is it like when God pampers you your way?

What is it like when God pampers you the way you want and need God to pamper you?

What is it like living in the environment you want and need to live in with God?

What is it like to have total peace – true peace here on Earth with God?

What is it like to just sit by the Ocean and or, Sea Shore and connect with God your way?

What is it like just sitting by the Sea Shore and or, Ocean having a mango with God your way?

Maybe my world is like a fairy tale with God like I said, but can God feel what I feel in this way?

If God feel what I feel even more, why am I here and not in the environment I need to be with God?

Why do I feel betrayed Life Wise? And I know betrayed is not the right word nor is lonely the right word. I am truly not lonely, but in need of a new and positive life change.

I truly need to live off the Grid of Man.

I need to live on the Grid of God. I crave this. More than yearn this; living on the Grid of God yet, God is truly not seeing this why?

Why do God leave my cravings and yearnings unanswered in this way?

For once I wish there was a true open door for me and God to commune with each other.

For once spoil me my way without limitations.

The wind is howling outside, and I have not taken my dog for a walk as yet. Belly hungry but I truly don't feel like eating anything. I truly do not care for food, but I have to eat something.

Going to walk my dog and hopefully later on today I will have more to write.

Michelle

Life can be beautiful
Life is what you make it

No, I so don't want to write today because I have nothing to truly write.

Just thinking of life and my surroundings.
Had things to do today but did not feel like going out.
Too lazy.

Want to take the bus but don't want to take the bus.

Aye yes, I wish I had a car.

Need to do some heavy praying on the things I need.
I wonder if God is going to hear me and grant me my true desires.

Building is important to me.
But how do I build me?

No, that's not it.

Do God truly build people?
Or
Do God shy away from building those that are truly true?

What is building to God?

Physical and Spiritual Building is truly not the same.

So why do God not build Physically and Spiritually true?

Meaning, why can't I see God truly building me.

Michelle
January 16, 2021

I've not been writing much as you can see because there isn't anything really to write about dream wise or other wise. It's January 17, 2021, and I've been dreaming safe dreams which is truly good for me.

MIXED RACE INDIAN DREAM

Dreamt this morning this Indian and or, Mixed Race Indians but I believe more of Africans but do not quote me. But Indian none the less whether mixed or not. Apparently different people were living with me. Anyway, this one Indian Lady and or, Girl found a two to three bedroom house. I can't remember if it was 2 or 3 but within that range. The rent she got the place for was $289.00. I was so happy for her because I could not believe someone rented her a house for that cheap in the highway 50 region in Brampton. She also told me she was going back home at the end of the dream. I cannot remember where – the land she was going back home to.

So, *I truly do not know if there is going to be a housing crash soon in Canada,* or if homes are going to catch on fire in Canada, or if it's only one home that is going to catch fire in Brampton. With her telling me she is going back home, I do not know if lands in Asia, Indonesia; lands that pertain to Indians, and Mixed Race Indians are going to be destroyed.

I just have to leave it alone. For me seeing Indians – Babylonian Indians usually constitute death of some kind.

I keep dreaming about my father.

When I called him yesterday, he was okay hence I am not going to worry about him. I am hoping I will go up next week to spend a day or two with him.

WARREN BUFFET DREAM

My other dreams not in any particular order had to do with Warren Buffet. Seeing him doing an interview about investments I was not pleased. Therefore, I did not watch the interview.

So, I do not know if something is going to happen to him in real life, life and death wise or if there is going to be a MAJOR STOCK MARKET CRASH real soon.

Further, I do not know with me seeing Warren Buffet if this is the signal for a Global Economic Collapse – Disaster and or, Recession. A Global Recession or just the United States going into recession. In all honesty, I truly do not care about the Billionaires of the World or if there is a MAJOR STOCK MARKET CRASH. The world needs this crash in my view. The only unfortunate thing about this; what is happening here on Earth is that the common folks – people are not seeing what's going on around them. All are conditioned to live and see things foolishly.

With this so-called pandemic people are not seeing that their fundamental rights and legal rights are being taken from them. For me, and to me; the world is moving towards Marshall Law. Humans are being controlled in some way, and it's not right what the governments, and some corporations are doing. My life hath worth and it's not right for any government or corporation to take that right from me. <u>Thus, I have to blame humans for the shit that is happening to us worldwide. We have absolutely nothing to gain but death and many are dying.</u>

Many are lied to.
Many kill to be apart of the world and realm of death.
Many can't live a decent life because life is taken from them.

Many cannot eat – do not have food because land space is taken away to build more concrete jungles.

The soil and landscape of Earth is eroding yet, we as humans are truly not seeing this. So, if there is a Global Economic Collapse then so be it. It is needed because humans cannot continue at the rate they are going.

WE CANNOT LIVE TO DIE.
WE HAVE TO LIVE TO LIVE. Therefore, we have to preserve life.

Yes, I know many cannot preserve life thus, the greed of the many and the few that take all today and leave tomorrow barren literally.

<u>JAMAICA DREAM</u>

This brings me to my other dream of me going to Jamaica and this Black Lady. I was talking about this pandemic and as usual, Blacks are ignorant and stupid when it comes to the lies they are being fed about this pandemic. I told her; this Black Lady, the cases will forever rise because the mask contribute to our poor, and ill health.

Our body was not designed to take in bad air, and breathe that same bad air. With the mask, it does not filter the air we breathe; we are still breathing the same bad air we are taking in. She walked away from me when I was telling her this. So, I truly do not know when it comes to Black People for real. They do not want to hear the truth from those who have the truth.

Lies suit many in our Black Community and this is so sad.

As Blacks, it's sad that we do not have our own Black Laws of Truth Globally that we are governed by. Instead, we are governed by lies.

We are governed by the lies the White Race and Other Races tell us, and give us.
We are governed by Religious Lies.
We are governed by Political Lies
Business Lies - Corporate Lies
Family Lies.
Historical Lies.
Educational Lies.
Systemic Lies.
Judicial Lies.
Martial Lies.
God Lies, and more.

THE SYSTEMS THAT WE HAVE IN PLACE GLOBALLY IS KILLING US, AND INSTEAD OF DOING ALL TO GET OUT OF THESE SYSTEMS OF LIES, WE STAY IN THEM.

I cannot talk or write anymore because I truly cannot see where Black People are going Future Wise apart from Hell.

We do not look into things because we are so accepting and conforming of all that is given to us.

Yes, you can say well what are you doing? And I am going to tell you. <u>OPEN YOUR EYES AND MIND TO THE TRUTH.</u> Those who know the truth and tell the truth are eliminated because they are educating you right.

QUESTION THE VALIDITY OF THOSE WHO SAY THEY ARE FOR YOU AND GIVE YOU DUNG TO EAT. If your pastor or political leader say kill, then question the validity of them.

If someone say, protest this, and this, then question the validity of them because they are putting your life at risk. Absolutely no one can fight for that which is wrong and get right. No, that's a lie, <u>people protest to stay in lies.</u> Want to be apart of the Lying Culture of Men and the different Races. Thus, the Global Marketplace, and the Political Arena Globally is run by lies and deceit. Thus, many are truly corrupt. A true government cannot have this set of laws for this race and that race in their country. Everyone must be governed by the same law.

Therefore, <u>THE LAWS OF GOD IS TRULY NOT THE LAWS OF MEN.</u>

<u>The Laws of Men are unfair and unjust.</u>

The truth is out there but you have those that will forever hide the truth from you including those Blacks in High Society that many of you look up to.

Those people are Bought and Sold therefore, they have to sell you the Devil's Agenda so that you cannot know – will never ever find out who they are, who you are; or know the truth.

It's time that Black People walk away from lies especially; Religious Lies, Political Lies, and the Educational Lies we are given. We as Black People need our own Black System that benefit all in society not just Blacks alone. But then, we will never have this being under White Rule, and the Lies Whites give us to live by daily. Thus, I ask; <u>WHERE ARE OUR BLACK LAWS?</u>

<u>HOW COME WE HAVE TO LIVE BY WHITE LAWS?</u>

ARE WE WHITE?
ARE WE NOT BLACK?

So, where are our good and true Black Laws for Black People to live by daily globally?

I am so tired of the fact that we as Blacks do not have our own <u>BLACK SOCIETY THAT IS BASED ON AND OFF THE TRUTH, AND TRUE TRUTH OF LIFE.</u>

I am so fed up THAT WE AS BLACKS DO NOT HAVE OUR OWN TRUE BLACK CULTURE THAT IS NOT BASED ON THE LIES OF OTHERS, AND THE DIFFERENT CULTURES OF OTHERS INCLUDING AFRICAN LIES. LIES AFRICANS TELL TO KEEP BLACKS GLOBALLY SHACKLED AND CHAINED TO DEATH – HELL.

I am fed up of the different systems in place that has taken Blacks from Life. Sick and tired of seeing – hearing how Blacks are killing Blacks in Black lands. Sick and tired of how we've been conditioned to hate self and each other.

Sick and tired of us as Black People not opening our eyes to our own Black Genocide Globally.

Sick and tired of our own inhibition – wanting to be accepted by those who truly hate us. Thus, they have all to gain here on Earth because we – Blacks have and has become the Sacrificial Lambs unto Death literally.

I am so sick and tired of us as Blacks letting other Races benefit off us, educationally, politically, religiously, life wise, death wise, law wise, God wise, and more.

I am sick and tired of us as Blacks sitting and waiting on their lying Messiah to save us when we as Blacks can do better for self and save self.

<u>WHEN WE BREAK AWAY FROM WHITE LIES; THE LIES WE'RE CONDITIONED IN, WE AS BLACKS WILL OPEN OUR OWN DOOR TO SURVIVAL.</u>

Blacks are not living. We are dying globally, and we still cannot see this.

You know what let me stop because in true truth, <u>I TRULY DO NOT SEE A BETTER TOMORROW FOR BLACK PEOPLE – THE BLACK RACE ON A WHOLE.</u>

Many are going to die with their White Counterparts and rightfully so because, <u>we allow others to sabotage our life.</u>

<u>We of our self sabotage our own life.</u>

We of our self want to live as the misguided.
We of our self like the lies we live and die by.

I cannot anymore Lovey. I know it is truly not going to get better for Black People Globally. You showed me what's to come thus, many Blacks are going to die Physically and Spiritually.

I cannot beg you for Blacks because <u>WE AS BLACKS REFUSE TO HAVE OUR OWN BLACK ECONOMY, BLACK LAWS, BLACK SYSTEMS OF TRUTH THAT IS TRULY INDEPENDENT OF WHITE LAWS, BIBLICAL LAWS, BABYLONIAN LAWS, AND MORE.</u>

So, if Blacks want to die in White Lies let them continue to die because many do refuse to listen. God, I am so sick of our stupidity period. Yes, I want to swear Lovey, but I am going to leave my anger alone and not let it overflow. <u>THERE IS A BLACK GOD.</u> *It is us as Black People that truly do not want our own Black God because if we did, Black People would truly not be here on Earth living amongst the heathens of life literally.*

Therefore, as Black; we have lost our COMMUNICATION with God literally. It's not we live we die. We are the ones that want to die thus, <u>LIFE; HUMAN LIFE HERE ON EARTH COMES WITH AN EXPIRY DATE FOR BILLIONS – ALL.</u>

There is so many things to do with Life and we are not taught these things. <u>Thus, the environment many of us are in contribute to our failure as Black People.</u>

Oh, come on you all know this and or, should know that; <u>THE ENVIRONMENT MANY OF US ARE IN – LIVE IN CONTRIBUTE TO OUR FAILURE AS BLACK PEOPLE.</u>

This is nothing new.

Listen this morning I was talking to God my way. I told God that God do not build people. He cannot build me.

In all I am doing, I am doing my best to build God so that you the individual can have an open communication with God so that God can help you, and add value to your life with value being, God adding Good and True Life to the Life you already have so that you can live not just here on Earth but in the Spiritual Realm. I told God I cannot stay with him, and I am not going to use him or her in this sense. <u>I told God I have to let him go because he cannot build me the way I need to be built.</u>

Listen I've told you. My life is like a fairy tale with God because I am expecting so much from God. Like you, I have difficulties with God thus, I hide absolutely nothing from God.

<u>I know my LIFE'S WORTH WITH GOD</u> but the things I need, God isn't giving it to me, and I didn't fully know why until this morning with this dream.

<u>MY DREAM</u>

Dreamt I had my place, and I can say this is an extension of the Babylonian Indian and or, <u>MIXED RACE INDIAN DREAM</u> I had, and told you about above.

My place was old, and renovation was going on on my building that I lived in.

Currently, at the time of editing this book they are working on my building. 2 water pipes broke.

In the dream, apartments were being refurbished – remodelled and they were beautiful – looked brand new with new glass. The apartments that were refurbished and or, re-modelled were gorgeous that I wanted one of the refurbished and or, re-modelled units. I had people living with me like I told you above. This one particular female that I know in real life was in the dream. I don't know what she did, but she did not want me to rise building wise I guess. No, not, I guess. She was holding me back from moving, finding a different place to live.

I had this brown dog with me, and I found her because I now know she did not want me to leave the apartment I live in to find better for myself.

Family and people, I got mad at her and told her she is evicted from my apartment, and her name was not on my lease. Trust me, the brown dog with me chimed in and told her off too. She was now sitting on the floor crying. She could not believe I evicted her from my apartment.

So as humans; *WE NEED TO KNOW THAT THERE IS TRUE SPIRITUAL WICKEDNESS OUT THERE.*

God is telling me, he is not hindering me from moving, someone in the living is hindering me, and blocking me from moving.

Listen people, there are people – physical and spiritual beings out there that truly do not want to see me rise in any way or fashion.

I am being blocked by Physical Evil and not just Spiritual Evil.

So, in life for some of us, no matter how hard we try to elevate, we cannot; *BECAUSE WE ARE BEING BLOCKED BY SPIRITUAL AND PHYSICAL EVIL – WICKEDNESS.*

SO MUCH THINGS TO SAY by Robert Nesta Marley aka, Bob Marley.

He did tell us about Spiritual Wickedness.

Listen, *Physical Evil is nothing compared to Spiritual Wickedness. Spiritual Wickedness is deadlier than Physical Wickedness – Evil.* Therefore, he Bob

Marley told you; *"he did not come to fight flesh and blood but spiritual wickedness in high and low places. So, while they fight you down stand firm and give Jah thanks and praises."*

Combating Spiritual Wickedness is truly hard here on Earth because Evil has free access and reign to Earth. Evil do come into Earth Spiritually and many people truly do not know this.

Spiritual Evil live in the Sky as well. This I know for a fact without doubt.

There is a lot that we as Black People refuse to accept because many of your ancestors were forced to relinquish the truth of what they know. Whereas; many – more than many was accepting of the evil they found – were conditioned and raised in. Thus, Black Magic for some, Obeah for some, Voodoo for some, Satanism for some, Science for some became the norm; apart of their culture thus, their religion. The Religion for some because the use of Negative Energy and Forces is involved, and still involved.

But in knowing this, and me evicting her from my home; God is supposed to be my greatest asset.

Why take so long to show me this evil?

Yes, I know the evils that hinders me, but you are God, build with me honestly and truthfully. All obstacles that are hindering me from living a good and true life with you, remove it. I should not have to tell you you are not a builder. I should not have to tell you as God I want to leave you because you are not building me the way I need you to.

No come on now.

This is wrong on your part. You have people that are there for you truthfully, why leave them in dismay? *Yes, I know my hindrance in life. I've complained to you about this for years, but this is 2021.* Do something to clear up the Physical and Spiritual Evils around me and the seeds you've given me. Yes, I know Earth is littered with evil – Negative Forces and Energy. I know these Negative Energy, and Forces weakens positive flow and Energy but come on now, you are my absolute truth and power. Negative Forces and Energy should not be around me or even hinder me from what I am doing come on now.

Yes, I am in the domain of the dead here on Earth due to the Sin and Sins of humans but if I cannot trust you to pull all the evil around me, who can I trust?

Yes, I now know what the Papaya Dream mean. I need to clean my insides using half a Papaya along with the seeds, and I have to do this because my Internal Organs need cleansing. Thus, I am looking into things I can use to clean my system out. I am not a fan of dried herbs. I am a greens type of girl so, I am eating a stalk of celery on the regular because I truly love celery. I am so going to use the Ginger, Celery, Pineapple, and Cucumber Combination to cleanse my Colon, but I want to incorporate the Papaya and Papaya Seeds into this mixture.

I need to also deworm my body in a major way. So, I am going to see and try Black Walnut Hulls and Wormwood.

I know they say Papaya Seeds is good for de-worming your insides. Hopefully, I will not be overdoing it. However, if I can incorporate Black Walnut Hulls and Wormwood just a bit with my Papaya, Papaya Seeds, Cucumber, Ginger, Celery, and Pineapple without over doing it I will, but I have to find out from a herbalist first and let you know.

I truly love cucumber, but I truly do not like or love English Cucumber. I prefer cucumbers with natural organic seeds.

So yes, there is a lot that Black People need to know when it comes to Good and Evil.

I need to learn to pull the evil forces and energy around me and God is so not showing me how to do this.

I cannot live in hindrance come on now. I am not getting any younger but older and as God, you cannot let your people and or, our people live in hindrance; lies. No one can reach you living in lies and denial come on now.

I am going to say this Lovey and truly forgive me. But, if you were truly true to me then all that hinders me in life will and would fall at the wayside. You would put up a more than impenetrable forcefield around me so that no form of Spiritual and Physical Evil can or will get to me, or stop me from doing pure and true goodness for you, me, and our good and true own; saved in life all around. I do not have your power but if the shoe and or, if I was you, I would protect you. No, I do protect you here on Earth. My truth for you is impenetrable. I cannot be rocked when it comes to you but with me, you allow evil to continue to take away my success.

It's 2021 therefore, evil must start falling.
Evil must come to an end.

Why show me true peace if we cannot have true peace here on Earth?

Why show me true peace if you did not want to live in true peace with me and the saved of life?

It's 2021 Lovey, I should not have to question you in this way. Things should begin to change for the better for me and you, and our good and true own globally come on now.

Evil cannot continue to rule this Earth therefore, Mother Earth need to step up her game to evict evil out of her come on now.

Lovey, why couldn't there be a better way for Black People?

Yes, I am hurting, and I know it's the choice we as Black People make. But Lovey, why can't Black People see you?

What do we know of you; our Black God which is you?
Why do we constantly give you up?

Finding you is bliss, but we as Black People have and has forgotten what we can do in a positive way when we have you.

You are my rely on Lovey despite me getting down on you at times.

Why is it as Black People we cannot see if we unify truthfully; come together truthfully as a collective we can <u>*CHANGE THE STRUCTURE OF EARTH TO BENEFIT US AS A RACE, AND PEOPLE POSITIVELY.*</u>

<u>*LORD GIVE ME STRENGTH*</u> – Luciano

If we were united truthfully wow – what we create would be truly unstoppable because we would have our power back to create, and garner true change here on Earth.

This we as Blacks truly do not know. <u>*Creation is possible,*</u> it is us as Blacks that do not want to create truthfully – properly.

Yes, it hurt to see Blacks killing Blacks.
It hurt to see Black Armies in Black Lands.
It hurt to see how corrupt some Blacks have and has become.
It hurt to see us as Blacks not instilling good moral values in our children.

It hurt to see us as Blacks not breaking away from our Colonial Slave Masters Law and Laws.

It hurt to see and know that hundreds of millions of Blacks are going to die.

It hurt to see and know that hundreds of millions of Blacks cannot see their Spiritual Hell they've created for self here on Earth.

Lovey, the pain is there. All I can say right now is truly hold on to me because I know the worst is yet to come literally.

How do I break the spell of ignorance that surrounds Blacks?
How do I open their eyes – the eyes of Black People for them to see and know?

How do I educate Blacks on the truth?
How do I teach them how to speak to you in truth?

Lovey, Blacks are going to die more. I know this, but we as Blacks have and has done absolutely nothing to try and save our self from what is to come.

Lands are eroding therefore, food shortage.
Global Climate Change, therefore; food shortage.
Earth is changing therefore, food shortage.
Companies building factories therefore, less farmland; food shortage.
Homes are being built therefore, less farmland; food shortage.

Governments allowing development of everything, and not preserving farmland for food thus; food shortage.

<u>I know there is another disease to come. Dear God when is enough enough when it comes to White Death; the White Race, and their destructive ways?</u>

Death a come
Death a come

Dear God; Black People Globally need to wise up.

Black People need to prepare, but how do we sound the alarm, so that those who are of life prepare and are truly not affected from what's to come?

Michelle

I so need to end this book. It's early morning January 19, 2021 3:48am. Earlier I was thinking about getting a spiritual bath and I went on YouTube to see if I could get some information.

Certain things I know already. I know about bath's and my grandmother back in the day use to give baths to people. Unfortunately, she never taught us – her grand children the art of bathing people, and pulling certain evils in your life, blocking evil, blocking the dead from sleeping with you, and more.

There were many things she could do but that was her gift and not mine. My gift is truly different.

I know certain things about baths but the full ingredients I did not know. I had an idea of what to use so you know what I am going to use my own knowledge. I never saw my grandmother using crystals, candles, or sea salts.

You know what let me leave it alone, but I truly do need a Spiritual Cleanse.

Connecting to my guide who is God is not an issue for me.
Connecting to the past of others is not an issue for me.

Seeing evil is not an issue for me.
Seeing into the future is not an issue for me.
Seeing into the Realm of Death is truly not an issue for me.

Connecting to the Moon is not an issue for me. The Moon is elusive. It's not everyone that can connect with the Moon and the energy, and technology source of the Moon. Some of you will not comprehend this but it's okay. <u>The Moon truly do not let you into its world just like that.</u> *This I know for a fact without doubt.*

Connecting to the Earth is not an issue for me. The Earth can connect with me which is great.

Connecting to Death is not an issue for me. This year I truly want to close off myself from Death because Death do take a toll on my body. I can feel Death; the Pangs and or, Sting of Death and this is truly not good for my body thus, I need to cleanse my Body and Spirit of all the Negative Forces and Energy that is bombarding it; me.

Cleaning my body of the Negative Forces is great but I also have to clean my room and declutter it. You cannot clean you – your spiritual you and space without cleansing your home of the Negative Forces that are in it.

My body is heavy – like led at times. Therefore, I have to now protect my body. I've not been doing this; taking things up in hand when it comes to me cleansing my body spiritually.

With God showing me her and what she did so that I cannot move, I have to do something for me. I do not have my grandmother around to show me what exactly to do and keep me safe from all the Negatives Forces that are around me as well as, the Negative Forces that come into Earth.

Listen, it's good to pray to God your way, but in all you do, you also have to do all to protect yourself from evil because <u>Earth is governed by evil.</u> Thus, evil do come into Earth. Evil do reside above in the Sky as well.

<u>To stray off topic. In Book One I said my Tab E I took to Cuba with me. I stand corrected. I did not TAKE MY SAMSUNG TAB E TO CUBA WITH ME. I TOOK MY PSP.</u>

<u>So, my Samsung Tab E never saw Cuba.</u>

I am thinking about cleaning my room, and I will find a way to clean it.

I am going to go back to bed because I have absolutely nothing else to write. Dream wise my world is fine, and this is good for me.

Michelle

MY TALK JANUARY 2021 – BOOK TWO

It is January 20, 2021, and I am so happy.

Walked both dogs yeah. My lower back is a bit sore but that's okay. Have some things to do on the road and I am hoping I can get them done.

Had a dream about my favorite Russian this morning and wow. Truly beautiful. Hopefully I get to meet him in person one day. Anyway, I did a Spiritual Cleansing Bath yesterday and today I am feeling a bit lighter and happier. In the bath I used, Sea Salt, Epsom Salt Lavender, Thyme, 3 Cloves of Garlic, 1 Lime, Sinclebible otherwise known as Aloe Vera to some, 2 small packets of Sage, and 1 packet of Rosemary that I got from Walmart, and some Florida Water Cologne.

I had my prayer with me that I wrote on my computer in Bradley Handwriting. I relaxed in the water and prayed the prayer I wrote for cleansing the evils around me. All that I needed for my cleansing and including my needs and wants I had on paper.

After praying, I put the paper in the water with me as I bathe – cleansed myself. Having the paper in the water with me was something I wanted to do, and I did it.

Trust me, in the water bathing myself and asking for cleansing of all the negatives around me, *I got in the spirit.* Not major because I did not want to go major. My children – 2 of them was in the apartment, and I did not want to scare them in that way. I can go off if the spirit takes me – grabs me fully.

So yes, I feel a bit lighter and different spiritually, but all is truly not done. I still have a long way to go cleansing wise. I do not follow the traditional route of cleansing because different people have different views. I know what my body need, and I try to follow my body. Certain things I do not know. *Sinclebible – Aloe Vera you have to be careful with in the Spiritual Realm because some do use this herb – Sinclebible for evil.*

It's weird because I checked my calendar and realized that I did this cleansing on the last day of Capricorn which is like yeah me.

Look, in life we all need to cleanse our spirit and for years I've been neglecting myself spiritually and physically. I can no longer neglect me because it is going to get worse here on Earth.

Everyone is looking for a better way when we of our self truly do not realize that we of our self can be a better way for us. There is so much that I see and know and I tell you these things within these books. In order for us to survive we have to know the truth, and we have to prepare for what's to come. *We can no longer live as the deceived. We can no longer live in hate because hate cannot save anyone nor will hate save anyone.*

Earth is changing and she must change drastically. The time of Death – Satan is up. So, because the time of Death; Satan is up, there must be a drastic change here on Earth when it comes to Good and Evil.

A change must come but it's not all that can or will be saved.

Not all is of life.
Many are of Death.
Many live for Death.

Therefore, many live to kill as well as, lie and deceive.

Humans truly do not think of their Spiritual Being – Self.

We do not think of that Energy inside of us that keep the Flesh – Body going.

This is why I started to tell you; <u>LIFE HERE ON EARTH COMES WITH AN EXPIRY DATE.</u>

It wasn't always like this, but unfortunately Life here on Earth has and have come to this. <u>*Human Life having an Expiry Date.*</u>

Once Human Life here on Earth have and has expired – the Spirit shedding the Flesh of Man – Humans; <u>then there is ANOTHER LIFE TO BE HAD DEPENDING ON YOUR SIN/EVIL, AND GOOD RECORD.</u>

This Sin/Evil and Good Record depends on the <u>LIFE YOU LIVE HERE ON EARTH.</u>

So, <u>THE LIFE YOU LIVE HERE ON EARTH DETERMINES WHERE YOU GO ONCE THE SPIRIT SHED THE FLESH.</u> And I've told you this in other books.

<u>*Absolutely no one can escape Hell if your name is written in the Book of Death.*</u>

<u>*Absolutely no one can go to Hell if their name is written in the Book of Life. Thus, know Life and Death. Meaning, know your Sin/Evil Record versus your Good – Life Record.*</u>

Do not listen to the church that preach lies on God. These people have absolutely no where to go other than hell. Now this takes me to this.

LOUIS FARRAKHAN

Louis Farrakhan wow because last year I wrote about the dream I had with this man. Thus, as Black People; it is imperative we know who oversee us, marry us, teach us, preside over our body once the spirit has and have shed the flesh, and more.

Some Black People who are amongst us, are truly not of God, but are the Agents of Death thus; Religion has and have billions. Meaning, have billions of you in Hell. Thus, your NAME IS IN THE BOOK OF DEATH WITHOUT YOU KNOWING IT. And please truly do not come to me with Jesus and your Jesus bullshit because I told you about Jesus in other books.

If you think Jesus died for you then that's good. This is your belief and true belief. Those of Life will tell you categorically without doubt that; NO ONE CAN DIE TO SAVE YOU, THAT PERSON HAVE TO LIVE TO SAVE YOU. NOR WOULD GOD LET A CHILD OF LIFE DIE TO SAVE THE WICKED AND EVIL OF EARTH. THUS, LIFE AND DEATH ARE TRULY NOT THE SAME.

God cannot save the Children and People of Death. God can only save the Children and People of Life.

God is not obligated to Death. God is obligated to Life.

For me, and some that know Life and Death can tell you of the demons that walk amongst us and pose as Blacks. These people are White and fall under the White Banner of Death thus, they must lie and deceive you in all that you do.

AS BLACK PEOPLE KNOW THE TRUTH OF ISLAM.

KNOW:
IT IS FORBIDDEN FOR BLACKS TO CALL THEMSELVES MUSLIM AS WELL AS, FORBIDDEN FOR BLACKS TO BE AFFILIATED WITH THE ISLAMIC KINGDOM OF THE GLOBE. This is because of Babylon and the Children and People of Babylon. Thus, know the truth of Egypt, and the so-called Exodus out of Egypt by Blacks in the days of old.

So, *this morning I am being reminded of Louis Farrakhan and his deceit. A true Agent of Death that has and have deceived many in the Black Community Globally.* This man truly do not know his hell. I did see his hell that I told you about in one of my 2020 books.

Trust me, **WHEN HIS SPIRIT SHED THE FLESH THERE IS NO PLACE FOR HIM TO GO BUT DOWN - HELL.** Thus, hell patiently waits for those who truly belong to hell literally.

This man is evil and trust me he will not get away with his evils he's done here on Earth because, all in the Islamic Kingdom Globally disrespect and disgrace Allah.

Every Muslim lie on Allah. Therefore, Allah know them not.

Many Blacks do not know that Allah is the shortened version of Allelujah.

ALLAH MEANS THE BREATH OF LIFE.

When the Spirit hit you a certain way you call out Allelujah. And anyone that violate life also violate and disrespect the Breath of Life. Therefore, there is many things that Black People truly do not know, and those Lying Africans refuse to tell the Truth of Life.

They keep the Colonized Blacks in the West in Slavery.
They keep you Shackled and Chained to Lies – the Lies of Slavery.
Thus, keeping millions of you in Hell.

As Blacks we cannot seek to get truth for the Lies and Wrongs of our past. It just cannot work therefore, **you NEED TO KNOW THE TRUTH AND FULL TRUTH OF SLAVERY, ISLAM, AND THE DIFFERENT RELIGIONS OF THE GLOBE THAT KEEP YOU CHAINED TO DEATH – LOCKED IN HELL LITERALLY.**

As Blacks we truly need to look into things. We have full access to God but none of you know this. Billions of you put your trust and all into false god and gods.

Listen and listen carefully, whether we like it or not, *Africa has all to gain Death Wise from You. Africa was where it all started for Death.* Therefore, Africans keep the Lies of Africa by telling you and selling you lies. *As long as you keep believing in African Lies, you cannot be saved.*

Once you believe in the Lies of Africa and the Lies pertaining to African Civilization then you have inherited Sin – African Sins – Lies. And for centuries Black People have and has believed these lies.

"NOT ALL BLACKS FALL UNDER THE BLACK BANNER OF LIFE." There are true Black Demons out there thus, "PHYSICAL DEATH – BLACK DEATH." Blacks that literally kill their own.

So yes, I know the Hell of this Demon that was/is planted by the US Government to lie and Deceive – KEEP BLACK AMERICANS TO LIES – DEATH.

Thus, you have many Black Sell Outs – Demons posing to be Black when they are truly not of the Black Race but of the White Race.

Yes, I want to swear thus; this FAKE ASS BC has and have sold – no, sacrificed many of you to Death literally.

But with all his lies and deceit *HE CANNOT SEE HIS HELL. BUT I DID AND DID TELL YOU ABOUT IT.*

Further know:
THE ISLAMIC KINGDOMS GLOBALLY HAVE AND HAS BEEN CURSED.

I TOO CURSED THEM. So, absolutely none in the Islamic Kingdom can see God or Allelujah – Allah who is the Breath of Life unless they have a true saving grace by a saviour here on Earth.

Babylon and the Children and People hath no saving grace with God or with the Breath of Life – Allah – Allelujah.

This has absolutely nothing to do with colour of skin but with God. THE GOD AND GODS OF BABYLON IS TRULY NOT GOD THEREFORE, IT WAS FORBIDDEN LONG AGO FOR BLACKS TO MARRY THE CHILDREN AND PEOPLE OF BABYLON. This has not changed from then until now.

Unless we as Black People know the truth, we cannot and will never be saved. We've been conditioned in lies and it's time we break away from the different lying systems of men.

For all you Blacks that have changed your birth name to an Islamic Name has and have sinned. Your name has and have been taken from the Book of Life and put in the Book of Death. God is not Babylonian.

God cannot change your name from your birth name to something else. If God did that; changed your name or allowed you to change your birth name other than through marriage, then God would have Sinned as well as, cause you to Sin, and God cannot Sin.

God do not associate self with anyone or anything who is not of Life. This I know for a fact without doubt. So, know the truth and stop being fooled.

Hence, <u>FOOLS DIE FOR WANT OF WISDOM</u> – Peter Tosh.

Anyway, I have to go on the road. Hopefully, when I get back in I can write some more but for now, have a good and blessed day. If I cannot write anymore, hopefully tomorrow I will write some more.

So, may your life be filled with true peace and truth continually without end.

Michelle

It is January 21, 2021 after 4am and I've been up for a little bit now. Daughter is up so I am not the only one up in the apartment.

Had a Fruit Bath yesterday and it was great. Skin felt soft and smooth after the bath. I wanted to do this because I am taking the initiative to clean myself internally and spiritually. I've been neglecting me people and the pain I was in last year and the years before that, I cannot take therefore, I have to take the initiative to heal and clean me.

I am hoping I find the right source that will help me physically and spiritually. All too often we think of the outer self – outer appearance and we do not think of our inner appearance therefore, <u>we neglect our internal organs.</u> So; as I grow, I am hoping that I will find all the right measures – cures to help me with my pain, internal organs, spiritual organs, and more.

Life is precious. It is us as humans that cannot see the preciousness of our life.

We put ourselves in situations we cannot get out of. Thus, Earth and the life we live here on Earth cannot be better for billions.

If it's one thing I know for a fact without doubt, <u>Evil do not want Good to succeed.</u> Therefore, Evil dominate Earth.

Evil dominates the life of some here on Earth.
For some they live for Evil because Evil is their God.

Some are controlled by Evil – demons thus, when they do wrong and get caught; they say Satan made them do it.

But in all I know. <u>Satan cannot tell anyone to kill.</u> So, people do lie on Satan as well.

See many do not know the difference between Demons and Satan.

<u>Demons tell you to kill. Not Satan.</u> So as Children and People of Life we have to know the difference between the two – Satan and Demons.

Demons egg you on.

Demons do control some because, some did sell their soul to death. Therefore, the demons that reside in them; some.

Some there is something called Generational Sins. Thus, demons are born here on Earth due to Generational Sins, and more. And yes, I am off track already. So yes, I had my fruit bath, and it made my body soft – smooth.

I do not have a set time for baths. I like to bathe in the evenings after 6pm but before 10pm.

So, I made a Parasite Cleanse Smoothie yesterday and it was delicious. I used ½ Papaya including the seeds – all the seeds of the ½ Papaya.

¼ Pineapple
1 sprig of Ginger

I made my own Coconut Milk by blending dry coconut in water. I did not use a half cup of Coconut Milk I used less. Used some of the Dry Coconut Water in the mixture.

I also used water. And I am telling you the Smoothie was blessed. It was not sweet, and I truly enjoyed it. I drank some and have some left over for today. I am trying different things to help my internal organs my way. I truly hope I can continue with this for the rest of the year and not fall by the wayside and give up after 3 or 4 tries.

What I did with the rest of the fruits was make a bath. I blended the rest of my Papaya with the Seeds, a sprig of Ginger – more than 1 tablespoon for me, ¾ Pineapple added Coconut Milk that I blended and some of the Dry Coconut Water. Added it to my bath water of Himalayan Sea Salt Pink. I made an oval shape with the salt. I found Lavender Fragrance Sachet and Orchid Fragrance Sachet at Dollar Tree. Man did I fall in love with the Lavender Scent. Trust me, when I have my own home somewhere, Lavender have to be in my garden because I truly love Lavender. So, I put about ½ Sachet of the Lavender in the water.

So, in my bath I had:
½ Papaya with Seeds
¾ Pineapple
Sprig of Ginger
Coconut Milk with a little bit of the dried coconut water
Himalayan Sea Salt
Lavender

I did not bring my prayer that I wrote with me from the day before. There was no need. I tried sitting in the water to soak but my legs would not allow me. I began to get muscle spasm and my knee began to act up, so I sat on the tub prayed and washed myself that way. When I was able, I stood up washed my body, including hair, face – all over. Again, I was in the spirit; which is good for me. I like being in the Spirit at times. With this bath I did not prewash – shower before. I did not want to, nor did I feel the need to. The bath was great, and my skin feels great. Just to note; during the bath my skin began to burn a little so don't be surprised if you get a slight burning feeling in your vagina area, your body, and head that lasts less than 10 seconds if you try this fruit bath. I did. My preparation bathroom wise was washing out the tub, toilet bowl, and wiping the floor. I do not use candles in that way. For me candles are for giving my room a beautiful scent, but I've not used Candles in a while. My kids use candles – scented candles on a regular though. Drying my hair and skin my hair, a part of my right arm, and chest began to itch. Nothing major but I was itching.

So yeah me, that bath is complete, and I am so going to do that bath again. It's a matter of when. Wow to how smooth my skin feels.

I so need to go back to bed but I do not feel that sleepy.

Now, the BOOK OF THE DEAD AND OR, THE BOOK OF DEATH.

I am so not going to get into this book right now because I cannot tell you all the names that is in this book nor the names that are being put in this book right now.

And please do not let anyone tell you that no one knows and or, can see into the Realm of Death, and no one knows the names of those who are going to Hell. I know so truly trust me on this one.

What I see some truly do not see.

If I tell you to prepare for the end would you do it?

Would you trust me to save you given all that I have written over the years?

Listen and listen carefully. It is only going to get worse for humans here on Earth. Some of you may already know this, but trust me, it is going to get worse. IT IS TIME FOR THE SAVED IN LIFE TO PREPARE FOR WHAT'S TO COME.

MANY MORE ARE GOING TO DIE GLOBALLY.

Why am I thinking about Bob Marley and Death?

Something is truly not right in the Marley Family.

Wow. I do not want to go off spiritually, but something is truly not right with the Marley's right now.

How do I put it with what I saw? <u>The names of humans are being put in the Book of Death.</u> You know what let me leave it alone because the end is near for billions globally, and I am so going to leave it this way.

<u>God did get the BOOK that was required of me. Therefore, I did fulfill my task; that which was required of me by God.</u>

Allelujah Death do speak literally.

Therefore, humans truly do not know what they've done here on Earth literally.

Wow. So, for you the saved in and of Life it's time to prepare for that which is to come globally. Many are going to flee to other lands, but the reality is; **ABSOLUETLY NO ONE CAN FLEE FROM DEATH.**

<u>It matters not where you run to – flee to; DEATH MUST TAKE YOU IF YOUR NAME IS IN THE BOOK OF DEATH.</u>

Humans cannot blame God or anyone for what is to come. IT IS US AS HUMANS THAT CREATED THE MESS WE ARE IN.

IT IS US AS HUMANS THAT TURNED FROM GOD.
IT IS US AS HUMANS THAT OVERPOPULATED THE EARTH.
IT IS US AS HUMANS THAT DID ALL TO KILL EARTH.
IT IS US AS HUMANS THAT DID NOT THINK OF OUR SINS.
IT IS US AS HUMANS THAT LIED ON GOD.

IT IS US AS HUMANS THAT PUT THE LIES OF RELIGION BEFORE SELF AND GOD.

IT IS YOU AS HUMANS THAT PUT POLITICAL LIES AND DECEIT BEFORE YOURSELF AND GOD.

IT IS YOU AS HUMANS THAT LISTENED TO THE LIES OF YOUR POLITICAL LEADERS THAT SAY GO ON THE BATTLEFIELD OF DEATH TO KILL, AND YOU DID. YOU AS CITIZENS WENT ON THE BATTLEFIELD OF DEATH TO KILL THUS SECURING YOUR SPACE AND PLACE IN THE CONFINES OF YOUR HELL – THE HELL YOU CREATED HERE ON EARTH FOR SELF.

THUS, HUMANS DID FORGET – THE WAGES – PAY OF SIN, IS DEATH.

Many did forget that the Physical and Spiritual is separate thus, all the ills you do here on Earth you must – have to answer for it in the Spiritual Realm.

Unless you are forgiven of your sins, and you have more good than sin then you cannot go up to see God – bypass your Hell. Thus, I tell you, and will forever tell you to know your Sin Record versus Good Record.

Each Sin comes with a penalty. See THE NEW BOOK OF KNOWLEDGE BOOK ONE AND TWO FOR THE DIFFERENT SIN PENALTIES.

So yes, Death is being written for humans – those who do not have their name in the Book of Life – God.

Listen, humans did not have to live this way. But humans did trust lies over God and now it's the end. The time of evil – Satan is up, and humans have to; must pay the consequences of all the lies they believe in and do.

Political Lies was/are not called for.
Religious Lies was/are not called for.
Generational Lies was/are not called for.
Family Lies was/are not called for.

In all humans did, humans live to die instead of living to live.

Humans did give up God. Thus, billions believed that Religion can and will save them, when Religion cannot save any. Religion was and still is Death.

Religion binds you to Death – Hell because Religion go against Life – God.

Religion tells lies on God – the True and Living God.

Now tell me, how can God give man – humans Laws to follow then go back on his word with the same Laws we are given?

God said, do not kill yet, God went back on his word by sending his prophets on the Battlefield of Death to kill. How does that work?

God wasn't God then. God broke his own law thus, making God a demon literally.

So, if God cannot keep his own laws humans cannot keep the Law and Laws of God. Therefore, know what you are doing. Thus, Religion is of Death.

Religion do turn you against God thus, taking you from Life – God.

I do not know when borders globally are going to be closed indefinitely, if they close indefinitely at all. But, ole people sey; <u>many a goh run tu di rock an di rock a goh refuse dem.</u>

So yes, many are going to run to God, and I am telling you this right now. <u>God is not going to hear billions.</u> Billions did turn against God and accepted Death as their Lord and Saviour.

I am so not going to go further with this because humans did make Earth the Prison for Physical and Spiritual Death. With Spiritual Death being you as a person handing over your life to Death.

No, not all handed their life over to Death hence many truly do not know about their generations – ancestral past literally.

As I look at the borders of the different countries globally. For me, people do not respect the borders of other people/nations. This is disheartening because I am one that refuse Evil Entry into my land. Whatever conflict your land is in with its citizens – meaning however you kill each other in your land is truly up to you. Do not seek asylum in my land because I did not put you in the situation you are in.

You put yourself in the situation.

You elected all facets of Evil – Dung to oversee you, and your land.

You as citizens of your land truly do not know how to live, nor do you know to live with each other in true peace.

Some of you want power and control.

Many of you di not go to God for righteous, truthful, honest, pure, truly peaceful, and obedient children, and more.

Money, greed, and evil was/is the mainstay of many.

So no, I refuse the Children and People of Satan – Evil access to my land and home with God once we have our home. Those who want better in life live better no matter how little they have.

MY TALK JANUARY 2021 – BOOK TWO

Like I said, <u>*many people live to kill.*</u>

<u>*Many people live to hate,*</u> and I refuse people like you in my land and lands with God thus, I ask God to separate Good from Evil here on Earth. No, lands do not have to be the way they are.

No one should have to live your evil way.
No one should have to live in fear.
No one should have to live to die.

No, I am closing off all God's borders to all facet of Evil. You chose evil for self, so die with Death. God and Life – Good and True Life was not your stay so now that it's the end of time; why should God save you? I forbid it.

When you were doing all your wrongs did you even think of Life; your Life in the future?

Did you think of your land and the other citizens of your land?

Did you think of God?

God anno puppunennay. Death is whom you gave your life over to and Death is going to take you to the Realm of Death. Thus, I saw the names being written in the Book of Death.

My concern is truly not your soul or you. My concern is for the Children and People of Life as well as God.

You created chaos in your land. Why the hell should another land accommodate you?

<u>Stay the hell out of my land. And if you come into my land by crossing my border, I am shipping your ass back home no questions asked. Do not disrespect my land because I truly do not disrespect yours.</u>

<u>We don't want your kind in God's Land period.</u>
<u>God don't want you, and I don't want you.</u>

And Lovey, forgive me of my forwardness. <u>No Lovey, how many here on Earth has and have invested in your Life honestly and truthfully?</u>

<u>How many get up and have a coffee with you?</u>

Thinking of coffee, we need to go for a coffee with each other soon, I'll buy.

What God has and have given me is for Our – the Children and People of Life only. Why the hell should I rob God and share with the heathens of life? People who are truly not of God.

Unnu jus want God when unnu hungry. Hell no. Let the god and gods unnu believe inna fine food fi feed unnu an gi unnu shelter.

Not even a tat of water would I give to the lots of you.

Satan and Death do not live in God's World come on now.

No Lovey and Allelujah. Look how much crap humans has and have done worldwide and at the last minute, billions are going to want a saving grace. *HELL TO THE NO. I AM CLOSING OFF ALL ACCESS TO YOU.*

No last minute stragglers. You've put absolutely nothing in Life yet, you want to be saved.

You did not know God, but at the last minute you want to be saved. You're gonna know God.

You don't have a good and true Bank Account – Life Account with God yet, you want to withdraw from God's Account. Hell no.

God's Account is truly not for the wicked and evil of Earth or anywhere for that matter.

What goodness have you done on the behalf of God and the Children and People of Life?

What goodness have you done for the Breath of Life?

God is not a joke. You can't use God because I will not let you.

Dyam wrenk.

Unnu noh noa Gad but unnu want Gad fi noa unnu.

Michelle

It's 7:40am. I did manage to go back to sleep and now I am awake again. I dreamt this older white guy. I will not get into the dream with him because he had a red book in his hand. Not many pages were in the book and someone said; I wrote the book, but I told him, *"I did not write the book."* The book was written by another Canadian Author; female Black Canadian Author. He showed me the inside of the book as well as the title, and the picture of the Canadian Author who did not look Black to me. She was very light skinned, and I believe her attire was more African, but I could be wrong. I wanted to tell him to hold on I am going to get one of my books and give to him, but I did not. We were at a conference you see.

I know there is war coming. I dreamt conflict amongst leaders. I can't remember if Beenie Man the Dancehall DJ was trying to squash the conflict by him telling the leaders; *"do you not see that people are watching; could see this, and if this is what they wanted people to see?"* So, I do not know what is going on in Jamaica politically, or what is going to happen to Beenie Man; if anything does law and or, conflict wise.

All I have to say is. There is no honour amongst thieves.

Every problem has a solution, but for Politicians – the Demons that oversee the citizens, there must never be any peace globally.

"DEATH MUST BE FED PERIOD."

Thus, you the citizens of the different lands globally are DEATH'S MEAT – FOOD.

"AND I SEE THE TEARS ON THEIR LIPS"

Dreamt one that looked like Djimon Hounsou. He was sitting down, and the setting was that of old. You saw the door of old and someone who you could not see asked the one that looked like Djimon Hounsou, *what did you see?*

Now in the dream Djimon had a chain around his neck. I cannot say he was shackled and chained, all I know is he had a chain around his neck like the chains some Africans wear around their neck.

The one that looked like Djimon Hounsou answered and said; *"AND I SEE THE TEARS ON THEIR LIPS."* I can't remember if he pointed, but I can clearly remember after he said that; *"and I see the tears on their lips,"* he closed his eyes, *and I thought he died* – the one that looked like Djimon Hounsou died. Oh man, I can't remember if Djimon Hounsou had a crown on his head as if he was a King.

So, from Africa to the Americas; North, South, and Central America I truly do not know what is going to happen.

"AND I SEE THE TEARS ON THEIR LIPS," tell me there is going to be a lot of people crying, and dying shortly.

I truly do not know what to say when it comes to the Djimon Hounsou dream because I do not know if this is a prelude to suffering – more suffering for Black People. And I cannot worry about Black People Globally because many – hundreds of millions – billions did accept death. The things you see Blacks doing now is more than hurtful. Therefore, I truly cannot worry about Africa and Africans because they do keep Blacks Shackled and Chained to lies especially the lies of Slavery.

Not one in Africa defend God therefore, Lies did come out of Africa.

Africa do keep Black Shackled and Chained to Death, and I've told you this in another book.

Listen, until Africans come clean with the truth, BLACK PEOPLE WILL NEVER BE BETTER. BLACKS WILL FOREVER EVER BE SHACKLED AND CHAINED, USED AND ABUSED – KILLED.

NATURAL MYSTIC by Robert Nesta Marley aka Bob Marley

He did try to warn us.

He did tell you "many more will have to suffer; many more will have to die."

It is us as citizens that did not listen to what he was trying to tell you in his songs. We keep ignoring things until things become too late. As people we cannot keep ignoring the warning signs of those who are trying to educate you truthfully.

God has tried.

God has been trying but we keep missing the warning signs of God.
We keep making the same mistakes over and over again.

How much more can I write, and people are not seeing – do not know?

How much more can I write and those who I've sent books too shut me down; truly do not help me to spread the message?

So how can you be saved if evil is preventing you from being saved?

MY TALK JANUARY 2021 – BOOK TWO

How can you know the truth if the truth is being kept from you?

Your life is truly not safe anymore. This I know.

Look at how you as citizens are shut down. Yet, developers are developing.

In the area I am in. Development is everywhere. Corporations are not shut down, but you the citizens are being shut down why? *Globally everyone is developing but none is preserving.*

But then, I did say; write in a couple of my earlier books. THE MENU IS GOING TO READ, "NOW SERVING HUMANS."

Now let me ask you this. WITHOUT FARMLAND, HOW ARE MANY OF YOU GOING TO EAT SHORTLY?

None is thinking of the Condition of Earth.
None is thinking of the Waterways of Life.
None is thinking about preserving Farmland.

None is thinking of the toxic waste, feces, and garbage that is being dumped on the Waterways of Life daily globally.

None is thinking of Life on a whole, and more.

STOP TALKING – Fiona

Truly listen to the lyrics of the song because nothing is changing for the better globally. And I am going to say this in this book. THE WHITE RACE HAVE AND HAS MESSED UP THIS EARTH *and every human globally has and have helped them; The White Race. The damage is done. Now tell me, HOW ARE THEY GOING TO FIX EARTH?*

Instead of fixing, they are causing more damage. Greed is and will always be the motivator of the White Race. Develop every square inch of land. Don't think of the future and future generations.

They; White People are so damned smart in their book, now look at their smarts here on Earth. So yes, the Devil did do their job thus, the irreparable damage they have caused, and done here on Earth.

Black People are no different. They too are so stupid that at times I have truly wonder about us for real.

Many Black Politicians sell off Black Lands to developers
Blacks too do not preserve land space for future generations.

Instead, Blacks have adopted this take all today lifestyle, and live greedy like their white counterparts.

WHEN YOU TAKE ALL TODAY. WHAT ABOUT TOMORROW?

Listen, I am all for Earth. And I am going to be cold right now. I AM GLAD EARTH IS NOT EXPANDING. I know for a fact without doubt Earth can expand. But I am TRULY GLAD SHE IS NOT EXPANDING.

WHY THE HELL SHOULD SHE CONTINUE TO GIVE WICKED AND EVIL PEOPLE A HOME IN HER? PEOPLE THAT DO ALL TO DESTROY HER DAY IN AND DAY OUT.

HUMANS ARE NOT JUST ABUSERS. HUMANS ARE KILLER AS WELL BECAUSE, HUMANS KILL EVERYTHING IN SIGHT ESPECIALLY THE GOODNESS GOD AND EARTH HAS AND HAVE GIVEN US.

So no, I will not cry for humans globally as to what's to come. Nor will I feel sorry for any Sell Out Blacks. We've raped our people enough, and now it's time for humans to pay for the sins they've done here on Earth as well as, pay for their sins done unto Mother Earth literally.

Humans need more than a wakeup call here on Earth because, humans are too evil and yes, I am hoping that God close all doors to all who wicked and evil people that will now call on Him God and or, Her God for a saving grace.

Preserve no one wicked and evil.

Preserve and secure the Good and True of Life but all who are evil preserve them not. Let them go down to hell because Hell was their good and true choice here on Earth come on now.

Yes, I want to write more but I am going to stop here for now.

Michelle

MY TALK JANUARY 2021 – BOOK TWO

Wow, January is winding down and I can't wait for the month to be over. It's January 22, 2021, and I dreamt all the worms in my body died.

I took a Parasite Cleanse as outlined above but that did not work for me on day one. So yesterday I added Black Walnut Hull and Wormwood to my Parasite Cleanse.

Boiled water and added ½ tablespoon of Black Walnut Hull and ½ tablespoon of Wormwood to one cup of boiled water. Made the brew stay there until it was cold; then I added ½ cup of boiled Wormwood and Black Walnut Hull to the Parasite Smoothie I made.

Wow to the bitterness. The bitterness reminds me of Bitta Gaul fi real to the bitterness of the brew.

Drinking 1 cup of this brew wow. My body felt so different because I could feel this crazy sensation throughout my body during the night. I did go to the bathroom during the night but barely anything came out, but my body feel so light thus, *I dreamt all the worms in my body died.*

I am going to finish off the Parasite Cleanse and again will add ½ cup of brewed Wormwood and Black Walnut Hull. Because I like to poop, I am going to take 1 capsule of Cascara Sagrada before I go to sleep and see if this will help me to get all I need out of my system poop wise.

Listen, you have to know what your body need, and our body do talk to us thus, your spiritual being. I like to experiment on my body to feel what work for me internally and physically.

I know my inside need cleansing. I just neglected doing what I need to do.

Trust me my body feel 100 pounds lighter right now. So, I am going to do a final cleansing for me because I need this for me and no one else but me.

Trust me, if I was in an environment that was warm, I would have my own organic - fully and truly organic farm. I would plant until I can't plant anymore. *Thus, at times I feel that I am in PRISON – HELL in the country I am currently living in.*

This country is my literal hell. I am truly limited environmentally and living space wise. So yes, I am bound in the hell that I am in – the land I am living in. Therefore, as humans; we need to know that some lands bound us to Hell. You see your need to escape but something has and have bound you to the land you live in so that you cannot rise; environmentally, space wise, food wise, housing wise, financially, God wise, and more. This is the way I feel for me thus, I need a true escape from North America literally.

FOOTNOTE:

I did not have a bath of any kind yesterday. I need to finish my Internal Cleanse first before I have another bath.

Also, DO NOT HAVE A HERBAL BATH THEN HAVE/TAKE A FRUIT BATH THE NEXT DAY.

Hear and listen: <u>DO NOT HAVE A HERBAL BATH THEN HAVE A FRUIT BATH THE NEXT DAY.</u>

<u>WHEN YOU DO THIS, YOU COUNTERACT THE EFFECTS OF YOUR HERBAL SPIRITUAL BATH.</u>

I needed to have a Fruit Bath. And yes, I did counteract the effects of my Herbal Bath with my Fruit Bath. Thus, yesterday my body was heavy – I was spiritually heavy.

So, know what you are doing.

So, as I journey though certain things, I am taking you along for you to know.

I am so listening to the <u>*TENAMENT YARD RIDDIM MIX*</u> by *Di Fyah Sound Crew*.

Wow to this Riddim. It is nice, and it gets you moving. Therefore, I so need a cutie to wine pan right now. Guh dey *Tanya Stephens* because a real <u>**BIG WOMAN TING.**</u> A big man mi love. Listen, I should stop because if I let my mind take hold of me; the things I would write that will make your eyes pop out fi real.

<u>*God, it's a pity Jamaica is deemed unclean by God because, I am missing my little island right now. I just have to stay my course with God fi now.*</u>

So off course because I wanted to say something else and now, I lost track because di <u>*TENAMENT YARD RIDDIM MIX*</u> a ole mi suh mi a figet wey mi fi write.

Okay, I am back now. If you are taking medications and want to try the Parasite Cleanse with the Black Walnut Hull and Wormwood, <u>PLEASE TALK TO YOUR HEALTH CARE PROVIDER.</u> Do not do what I do without getting all the right information. I know my body and what I can and cannot do. See the window you have when it comes to Medications taken and Herbal Remedies you want to take. Meaning, you can take certain Herbal Medications 3 – 4 hours after you've taken your Prescription Medications, so know your window. I am seeking Naturally Organic Herbs to help me combat my Health Issues. The More I learn is the better it is for me because I truly loathe pharmaceuticals. Therefore, as humans it is imperative for us to guard our Internal Organs.

Pharmaceuticals are not the best preventative medicines in my view. Yes, many will dispute this; my words, but you are entitled to your opinion, and I cannot wrong you for your views. Your views and opinion are yours thus, Freedom of Speech.

Listen, if I could live truly organic then I would be truly happy because I know I will be connecting to God, and Mother Earth and or, the environment I live in positively. I would have no care in the world because I truly crave and yearn to live <u>OFF THE GRID OF MAN – MEN.</u>

I do take Pharmaceuticals but trust me, I cannot wait for the day when my body, mind, and spirit shout Allelujah I don't have to take the different pharmaceuticals, and just praise God. My body, vibration, and more is in synch with God, and all the good and true vibes and vibrations of life.

<u>Listen and know:</u>
<u>NOT ALL YOUR AILMENTS IN LIFE IS PHYSICAL. YOU DO HAVE SPIRITUAL AILMENTS THAT CONTRIBUTE TO YOUR ILL HEALTH.</u>

This is why you need to clean your spiritual being as well as, your living space spiritually and physically.

Know, the dead can sleep with you as well as, have sexual intercourse with you. So yes, you have to guard yourself in life when it comes to certain things.

Got to go and hopefully later I will be able to write more, but if I cannot write more, I will try to write something the next day.

Michelle

Did what I had to do, and my muscle spasms started to act up. I was getting a break from it and now here we go again with the severe pain.

Went to the store and got what I needed and to my shock when I got home, I realized I had absolutely no lower back pain. I walked without pain. This is fantastic but not so fantastic with my muscle spasms. It seems when it's not one thing it's the other for me. Managed to get to the washroom in my room and used a hot rag on the areas that were bothering me. Googled foot pain.

I know where my pain is and how it starts but what I am looking for is the correlation between your Feet and Muscle Pain if I am making sense word wise.

I don't know but to me the foot is a pivotal point for me when it comes to your nerves – Spiritual Well Being in some way. Our overall well being for me start with the Spirit and without the Spirit we have not life thus we get sick and die. Thus, a lot of things we do including consume affect our Overall Physical and Spiritual Well Being.

Looking at a Foot and or, Feet Schematic, I know where my pain points are on my right foot.

My pain points are 6-10 on the Foot Schematic.

- *6) Intermediate Cuneiform Bone*
- *7) Medical Cuneiform Bone*
- *8) Metatarsal Bone*
- *9) Proximal Phalanges*
- *10) Distal Phalanges*

I am going to leave out the Navicular Bone because I saw this on another Schematic.

Every part of our body is essential to life, and for me I am on a journey to learn more about my body and how I can keep my body vibrating optimally in a positive way so that I am not affected and or, my body can reverse the damage already done to it.

Spiritually it is possible.
Physically it is possible.

Herbs, plants, food, water, exercise, meditation is important to good vibration. But I cannot vibe because my brain truly do not want me to vibe in the way I need to thus, higher learning.

I am so not going to get into higher learning in this book because I know what I need. Getting there is the difficult task because I cannot connect to people that are like me in that sense that seek and need more than true peace if that makes sense to you.

There is a better way of life out there, but connection wise I am lacking the knowledge to get there. Thus, TRUE KNOWLEDGE, TRUE AND PROPER LEARNING IS KEY TO LIFE.

Without the truth we are dead. And billions are literally dead.

Thus, I tell you, I truly do not want or need to live off the Grid of Man – Men. I need to live on the Grid of God.

Knowledge is power for some. But in true truth; knowledge is also CREATION.

And yes, for you who think I do not see the word Cuneiform I see it. Thus, Cuneiform is an ancient language that is based off Sanskrit.

Sanskrit is the original language of Babylon thus Hindi, Urdu, Arabic, Hebrew, Farsi – the different languages of Man – Humans.

God has a language, but it's not many that can write the language of God. I know if I did; know how to write the Language of God many things I would not be complaining with God about. I would be able to help myself physically and spiritually.

When you can write the Language of God, you have certain power.

There's a lot you can do to shut down evil, plus, do a lot more.

Listen, there is so much to learn, and I am going to leave things as is right now. Hopefully as I grow good with God, you are there with me growing good and true as well.

Listen, it is good to learn about herbs and how the different herbs help your body, but you need to know how your feet work as well.

I am so going to leave off now. I need to find certain things and it's hard for me when I am walking alone on my journey. I cannot find people that share the same views; no, not views; but knowledge as me.

Need true Zionists that are true and clean spiritualist around me.

Michelle

Yes, it's January 23, 2021 and January will soon turn into the Month of Truth – February. Looking forward to February because it's Black History Month, the Month of True Love, and more,

I was supposed to do a Final Parasite Cleanse using my Parasite Cleanse Smoothie and Black Walnut Hull and Wormwood, but I could not do it. My body revolted at the thought of the Bitta Gaul taste. Plus, my Smoothie did not taste right therefore, I did not finish it. Before I went to bed, I took 2 Cascara Sagrada Capsules. It tasted bad in my mouth, but I was so disappointed in the effect of it.

You know when you are gearing up for this massive poop effect where you poop out a billion pounds of toxins in your system. Yes, I know I am over exaggerating, but I thought I would poop a lot but no. Poop did not fill my toilet boil. Do not feel different or anything like that.

Yes, this is the weird me. Yes, I know everyone's body is different and my body is one of those difference. It's not like when I drink beet root, ginger, carrot, and celery combined where wow to my pooping.

Laugh because this is me. I am open and honest with you in all I do. Therefore, I take you on my journey with me. Hey, I am still listening to *Big Woman Ting by Tanya Stephens come on now.*

2021 is my year for change and I am doing it. Changing me health wise because I truly need to help myself. I know what I need, and I am doing it. So as the months change, the days change, and time; the time of man – humans change, I have to make a positive change for me.

I have to consciously do for me, and I am doing it.

Today, I am trying thyme, ginger, and cranberry tea. I have a lot of mucus build up in my body and I want to get rid of it. I truly hate so much Mucus in my body. Just gross therefore, I am hoping with all the experiments I am doing, I will find the right remedies for me.

Hey, I need to look sexy and neat for the summer for me honey. I've let my body go for far too long and I am an extremely big girl. And yes, I am proud of me.

There is absolutely nothing wrong with being big. I just need my fitness to get back to normal. Hey, I need to *JOOK START MY LIFE MY WAY. Therefore, as Tanya Stephens say. A REAL BIG WOMAN THING.*

Yes, it's unfortunate Jamaica is off my radar because, never mind.

Some Jamaican man love di fluffy dem. Yeah, <u>MY REAL AND TRUE JAMAICAN GUY.</u>

You know what let me get back on track because again, with this song, my mind is racing in a different way.

Seriously, I truly do not know what is going to happen in the heavens – sky.

Yesterday, I was seeing this child – the same one I wrote about in Book One before me. This child has become apart of my waking state visions.

I so can't remember if I saw turmoil – fighting – brutal fighting in the WWE. This only mean someone in the WWE is going to die. There are no ands ifs or buts about this. It's a matter of who dies.

<u>Oh, Himalayan Sea Salt for me. Body is so against it so. So, I will not be using this salt ever again.</u>

RUSSIAN FASHION INDUSTRY DREAM

I do not know where to begin. It was like I was at a gas station at Keele and Sheppard. There was this Young Russian Female Designer and this young child no more than between 8 – 12 years old.

The 8 – 12 years old spoke something in Russian. She was showing off on being a model because she was a very beautiful child. Oh man I can't fully describe this child. I am not 100 percent sure, but I think she had blue eyes, and brown hair. She was well done up for a child.

She was happily showing off and the Young Female Russian Designer said something to her, and like magic changed her attire – dress to a sequin dress – red sequin dress that was below her knees.

Red dresses usually mean someone is hiding something. <u>Therefore, when it comes to CHILDREN IN THE FASHION INDUSTRY GLOBALLY SOMEONE NEED TO DELVE DEEP INTO THIS INDUSTRY.</u> Someone is hiding something globally when it comes to kids being used and abused in this industry globally. Hence, you have sick bastards that use and abuse kids. And, you have their disgusting parents who turn the other cheek, and watch their children suffer because of a damned paycheque; hush money, blood money, child molestation money, and more.

Therefore, some parents should not be parents. Money takes precedence over the life and lives of their children literally.

So yes, humans do all to destroy. Not even the parents of some care for real. And these monsters you want to save in life Lovey? No, you would not be a God of goodness and truth if you save creatures – demons such as these.

After seeing that and continuing with my dream. Something was said and I took off my socks, and cockroaches came out of my socks and got on the ground in the grass. I could not kill them. This medium size one and small ones got away. Mind you, I had another pair of socks in my hand that I could put on.

That part with the cockroaches I truly do not know what that means.

Cockroach dreams I truly do not know what they mean or represent.

Drinking my thyme, ginger, and cranberry tea. So, I am hoping to get rid of some of the mucus in my body as well as clear up my urinary tract. If this remedy helps, then yeah me. I will tell you all about it.

I used about 10 sprigs of thyme, 14 frozen cranberries, a sprig of ginger. Boiled in 1 cup of water for about 5 minutes well until the water began to boil. I did not time this brew. Poured into my cup and I made the brew sit until lukewarm, and now I am drinking my brew.

This is me for now until I stop – get lazy and go back to the old me of laziness and unhealthy living and eating. Right now, my body is my experimental guinea pig.

Wow, I can't eat the cranberries. Ate about 4 – 5 and they are slightly bitter and tart.

Tummy feels weird now. And I am so going to lay down.

Did lay down and played my games and about 1 – 2 hours. And yes, I did poop the poop I wanted to. Had energy to clean my washroom and my lower back did not give way. I was able to bend the way I needed to bend. Have not bent like that in a while. So yeah me. I am going to continue with this regiment but not everyday. What was even more amazing for me was that; I was able to take a shower and not have to worry about my back. Lower self in a way where my back would not hurt me pain wise. So yes, I am going to see where this lead me lower back wise. Tomorrow is another day and we will see.

Michelle

MY TALK JANUARY 2021 – BOOK TWO

STOP THE FIGHTING RIDDIM mixed by Banton Man

Truly like this riddim because what is happening in Jamaica and Globally it truly not necessary.

I am so sick and tired of the demons that run – control this Earth.

I truly do not know why humans cannot see that the evils they do here on Earth seal them in Hell.

Look at a dead body. That dead body cannot face hell and will never ever face Hell. That energy – your spirit and or, soul for some is what must face hell literally. Trust me; for those who truly do not know the truth is hell bound, and they cannot blame anyone but self.

Thus, my dreams this morning. *Black and White People Globally, not one of you will escape your judgement because things have and has been written in the Spiritual Realm thus, Isiah of your so-called holy bible was given unto to you as well.* Meaning, Isiah is for all globally to read because Death is going to walk more and more here on Earth.

BLACK MAN DREAM

Dreamt this Black Man. I do not know where we were, but this rectangular table was set, and books were set on the table. Hard Cover books. Think hard cover books like text books.

This Black Man asked me a question about, *"DISCIPLING OUR CHILDREN."* I said; look, and I turned two books over to reveal the back of the book and the picture of two people. One (1) book cover was of a Black Man that would resemble Lionel Ritchie, and the other book cover I turned over was of a White Man. I said to him, *"we are not White we are Black, and we cannot discipline our children the White way."* He went a little further into history and was talking about how White People came in existence. *He knew the Origins of THE WHITE RACE.* I wanted to elaborate further with him regarding the Black Female Genealogy, but I did not. I woke up out of my sleep leaving things as is.

So yes, you do have Black People out there that know the Genealogy of Blacks but keep their mouths shut and this is truly a shame. I am going to say this again.

UNTIL AFRICA – AFRICANS START TELLING THE TRUTH, BLACKS WILL FOREVER EVER BE SHACKLED AND CHAINED TO HELL.

African Lies are hell. Our death trap literally therefore, <u>AFRICA MUST DO THE RIGHT THING AND TELL THE TRUTH.</u>

Listen, <u>EVIL DID NOT INVADE AFRICA JUST LIKE THAT.</u>

<u>BLACKS OF OLD DID SELL OUT – WALK AWAY FROM GOD.</u>
<u>BLACKS OF OLD DID PRO-CREATE WITH EVIL.</u>

And yes, I truly do not care if you don't believe me. <u>KNOW THE TRUTH. WITHOUT TRUTH YOU WILL NEVER EVER KNOW LIFE – GOD. NOR, WILL YOU BE SAVED FROM WHAT'S TO COME.</u>

<u>BLACKS OF OLD DID WALK AWAY FROM GOD. When we as Blacks walk away from God, GOD LEAVE US TO THE SIN AND SINS WE'VE ACCEPTED IN LIFE. THEREFORE, ONCE GOD DIVORCE YOU THAT DIVORCE IN MORE THAN INFINITELY AND INDEFINITELY.</u>

Know that when you divorce God – Life, Evil can take your history and replace your past history with whatever they want to.

How do I put it?

You become the PROPERTY OF EVIL.
Your children become the PROPERTY OF EVIL.
Your land become the PROPERTY OF EVIL.
Your wealth, artifacts; everything become the PROPERTY OF EVIL.

So, however evil use and abuse you is truly up to the Children and People of Evil.

Mother Africa did open up her garden to evil.

Mother Africa did pro-create with evil. So, because of this, WHAT MOTHER AFRICA DID, HER PEOPLE – BLACKS HAVE AND HAS BEEN COLONIZED, USED, ABUSED, ENSLAVED, AND MORE.

Therefore, know.

<u>WHEN YOU ACCEPT EVIL IN YOUR LIFE, IT IS VIRTUALLY IMPOSSIBLE TO GET RID OF EVIL OUT OF YOUR LAND, AND LIFE.</u>

<u>YOU THE PEOPLE BECOME THE BITCH OF EVIL whether you know it or not. THEREFORE, UNTIL AFRICANS START TELLING THE TRUTH BLACKS GLOBALLY WILL NEVER EVER BE FREE.</u>

I am getting pissed.

<u>AFRICA – AFRICANS TELL THE BC TRUTH MAN COME ON NOW.</u> You cannot keep the Lies of Satan and their people anymore.

Blacks are dying.
Blacks are living in sin.

More Blacks are going to die in lies and ignorance.

You cannot continue to keep Blacks shackled and chained to Death. Hell is truly not pretty, and you have an obligation to your people.

No, because my anger is flaring.

<u>WHY THE BC, and F word do you as a people continually sabotage BLACK LIFE?</u>

Why, you like to see your own Blacks Die?

<u>Do you think in Death – Satan is going to have compassion for the lots of you?</u>

Satan cannot save anyone from Death. All Satan can do is hand you over to Death.

Look at Africa today and tell me if any of you are better.

<u>KNOW THIS:</u>

<u>ONCE BLACKS FAIL GOD GLOBALLY NOT ONE BLACK ON THE FACE OF THIS PLANET WILL SEE GOD. Trust me, hell will be unleashed on every Black globally.</u> This I know for a fact without doubt.

<u>THERE IS NO JESUS TO SAVE YOU. YOU WOULD HAVE FAILED YOU, YOUR PEOPLE, GOD, ALL LIFE. THEREFORE, IT'S TIME FOR ALL OF AFRICA TO TELL THE TRUTH BECAUSE, IF ANY OF YOU THINK SLAVERY IS OVER TRULY THINK AGAIN.</u>

<u>BLACKS ARE THE GLOBAL TARGET MARKET FOR DEATH.</u> You cannot dispute this. So, stop lying to your Black Own. <u>You are original therefore, EVERYONE THAT IS ORIGINAL HAVE THE TRUTH.</u>

ABSOLUTELY NO ONE OF LIFE CAN HIDE THE TRUTH AND KEEP THE LIFE OF DEATH. THEREFORE, I DO SCRUTINIZE YOUR GENEALOGY for real. <u>TRUE BLACKS CANNOT KEEP THE COUNCIL OF DEATH IN THEIR KINGDOM PERIOD.</u>

As Blacks we can no longer fight for evil.
We can no longer fight to stay in evil's domains.

Blacks need life. Therefore, Blacks have to break away from evil.

<u>I am going to go as far as saying this. IF AFRICANS TRULY LOVED THEIR BLACK OWN - BLACK PEOPLE GLOBALLY, THEY WOULD TELL THE TRUTH AND NOT KEEP ANY BLACK PERSON SHACKLED AND CHAINED TO HELL WITH THEIR LIES.</u>

If Africans truly loved their Black Own:

<u>AFRICANS WOULD NOT KEEP THE LIES OF DEATH.</u>

<u>AFRICANS WOULD NOT DO ALL TO KILL YOU AS BLACKS WITH THE LIES THEY TELL AND TEACH; KEEP.</u>

Listen to me and hear me.

<u>KNOW THIS:</u>
And yes, I did tell you this in other books. <u>WHEN YOU LET EVIL OVERSEE YOU, YOU TAKE ON THE SINS OF THAT EVIL PERSON THAT OVERSEE YOU.</u>

Listen, <u>God is with no Church or Clergy.</u> So, <u>if you go to church and your Pastor preach to you, preside over your dead body, marry you, and more, you are taking on the Sin and Sins of your Pastor.</u>

So, if you had 1 sin on your Sin Record and you let a Pastor preside over your dead body, marry you, preach to you, christen or, baptize your child, and that Pastor had let's say:

116 667 666 000 000 000 000 000 sins on their Sin Record. You, including, your child and or, baby has and have inherit the sins of your Pastor. Your Pastor have and has inherited your sins as well.

Now, that sin amount of 116 667 666 000 000 000 000 000 is not served in Physical Time. That sin is served in Spiritual Time. Thus, your spirit have to spend all that time burning in hell if you have more Sin than Good on your Sin versus Good Record. This is why I tell you, know your Life and Death Record.

So yes, when you accept the lies of Africans; YOU TAKE ON THE SINS OF AFRICA AND ALL HER PEOPLE. Listen, not one you cannot add up the Sins of Black Africans Globally thus, it was ordained for BLACKS TO FAIL LIFE.

Thus, the Lies of Jesus hundreds of millions if not billions of you believe in. thus know, LIES DID COME OUT OF AFRICA.

Further know:
Not all Life - Black Life originated in Africa. Blacks we in Europe, Asia, South, Central, and North America. Everywhere on Earth you can think of; Blacks were there. So truly do not buy into the ALL BLACKS CAME FROM AFRICA BULLSHIT.

Blacks were in India, Pakistan, the Middle East long before Babylon came along. So, know the truth because; the HISTORY BOOKS OF MAN IS WRONG - FALSE when it comes to the origin, and origins of the Black Race.

Africans cannot tell the truth because, AFRICANS TRULY DO NOT KNOW ABOUT CREATION.

Therefore, know the difference between Creation and Pro-creation. With creation being those who were born without the fusion and or, union of Egg and Sperm.

If Africans truly loved you as Black People, none in Africa would condone Politics, Religion, the lies written about Blacks in the different Books of Men.

If Africans were original, none in Africa would allow the Devil's Agenda, and Systems in their land.

If Africans WERE LOYAL TO THE TRUE AND LIVING GOD; OUR BLACK GOD, ALL OF AFRICA WOULD DEFEND THE TRUTH OF GOD UNTIL THIS DAY.

Many of you as Black People need to think and know that; NOT ALL BLACKS ARE BLACK. MANY BLACKS FALL UNDER THE WHITE BANNER OF DEATH. THUS, THEY ARE WHITE. *Truly loyal to White Death therefore, they have to take you to hell with them. Death is their true agenda therefore, they have to;* must SERVE DEATH.

Therefore, all you've been taught about Colour of Skin is false, a damned lie.

You know what let me stop because if I continue, I will all out CURSE ALL OF AFRICA, AND NOT CARE WHAT THE HELL DEATH DO TO RAVAGE THE LAND.

No, I am not that sinful because I know God has wonderful things instore for the Southern Lands of Africa.

No People, it does hurt me to know that Blacks has and have done so much yet, we of our self has and have sabotaged our life by accepting crap of shit to live by.

Wrongs are wrongs.

ABSOLUTELY NO ONE CAN GET RIGHT FOR THE WRONGS THEY HAVE DONE.

Listen, I know for a fact without doubt; DISOBEDIENCE OF GOD IS AUTOMATIC DEATH. So, once your time here on Earth has expired then your time – Spiritual Hell begins. And it matters not if you cremate your body here on Earth. Absolutely no one can escape Death if their name is in the Book of Death. Therefore, know the truth.

So yes, all who follow behind their evil Political Leaders – you who voted for them, kill for them – your evil Political Leader. Know for a fact without doubt you cannot be saved. Hell is your home.

Look up and see the Sun that warms up Earth. Your Spiritual Fire is hotter than the fire of the Sun you see. Your spirit can go through the fire of the Sun, but your Spirit cannot go through the Fire that consume your Spirit. So, for Billions, <u>hell is truly their home literally.</u>

Listen, as it is. <u>I truly do not want or need to be anyone White right now.</u>

Wow, because; none in the White Race is thinking of their hell when their spirit leaves the flesh behind.

Laade Gad what a lala when dem fine out di penalty - time they are going to spend in hell.

Laade ooh, because all you've done to Blacks and the Different Races Death truly love the lots of you. <u>All the evils you do here on Earth is to secure your place in hell, and none of you know this.</u>

So, no, I know the Death and Hell of many in the White Race thus, <u>I KNOW, AND HAVE SEEN SATAN IN HIS BURNING STATE IN HELL LITERALLY.</u>

Michelle

DWAYNE "THE ROCK" JOHNSON AND BIG SHOW DREAM

I already told you there was death coming in the WWE. Now yesterday January 25th I dreamt the Rock; Dwayne "The Rock" Johnson, and Big Show.

I believe the Big Show and the Rock had an altercation wrestling wise but don't quote me. I cannot fully remember. What I do remember is seeing the Rock and his youngest children in a grocery store, and the Rock was cashing out his groceries. The bill was a bit high and he said, *"I always pay my bills"* as he was in disbelief of his grocery bill.

Now the Big Show was at my home and I had Sinclebible – Aloe Vera about ¾ left over on my table. For which I do have in real life. In the dream the Big Show took my Sinclebible – Aloe Vera. I tried to get it back from him, but he pulled it away from me. I had to tell him that was not nice, he could have caused the pricks on the Sinclebible to cut me, and he apologized.

I am not going to analyze this dream. All I can say is all who have signed on the dotted line and or, Line of Death cannot be saved. You cannot sell your soul and or, make sacrifices onto Death and think that you are going to live. And I am going to leave it at that.

Now this morning January 26, 2021 I am dreaming about guns. White People fighting – like in a movie and killing each other. Somehow Arnold Schwarzenegger was in the dream. He got hit by with a bullet and you could see this blue liquid in his chest. Think Iron Man. They pulled this metal out of him just like in Iron Man. So, I do not know if he's going to do a movie pertaining to the same theme and or, if they are going to resurrect his robot – Terminator movie.

Still after seeing that, people kept fighting. So, with that said, I do not know if fighting is going to erupt from Europe to the Americas, but I did tell you about what I saw in regard to the Blood and Cripts in Book One.

So yes, most of my sleep dream wise was not good. It was filled with fighting. Thus, many humans live to kill – destroy. This is their job. They live for Death therefore, they have to kill for Death.

DIANA ROSS AND ANITA BAKER DREAM

Now not too long ago as it's almost 9am, and I am writing. I dreamt, *Diana Ross and Anita Baker.*

Both ladies were singing, and I wanted to say Old School meets New School in the dream but could not. Both ladies are Old School Singers. Everything about the ladies was wow for me.

The main focus of the dream for me was not Anita Baker but Diana Ross.

I was so wowed by the way Diana Ross looked. She was so young in the dream that I could not believe she was so young. *When she finished singing, all I saw was this yellow electrical light around her head, and the wig she was wearing fell to the ground.* She did not know her wig fell to the ground, and her natural kinky hair was showing. I am going to put a measurement to her natural kinky hair of about 6 – 8 inches in length.

I cannot fully analyze this dream because, I do not know if this dream is for her and or, her children and or, grand children due to how young she looked in the dream. All I can say is she as well as, *her children and grandchildren have to safeguard their health stroke wise, heart attack wise; health wise.*

As for Anita Baker, I cannot tell you anything. *Black clothing is death for me.* So, I do not know if someone in her family is going to die. And no, I cannot tell you the song, or songs these ladies were singing. You saw them on stage, but you did not hear them singing. Oh man, I can't remember if a young white male and female was with me. *No, a young white female, and a young white male was with me in the dream.*

I know Diana Ross have White in her family, but I do not know if Anita Baker does. So, the White Side and or, White Family Members of Diana Ross have to be mindful of their life – health as well. All around all have to be mindful for of Strokes, or a Brain Aneurysm. Just guard your health please.

SHAQUILLE O'NEAL DREAM

Dreamt Shaquille O'Neal as well.

His dream was like a television show. A Black Family was doing a television show and I was seeing it. Shaquille O'Neal came in. You know what. Let me leave this dream alone because in the dream Shaq was different. *His aura, and all around Shaq was not beautiful. He was ugly to me thus, wow.* Let it go Michelle.

Listen, no, leave it alone. One red glass, one clear glass, alcohol – Vodka. Clear Glass was put into a Red Glass. Thus, Shaq, know that *EVERYTHING THAT IS HIDDEN IN LIFE MUST COME TO THE LIGHT. Absolutely no one can hide anything from God or Death.*

Trust me, *YOU ARE THAT SPIRITUALLY POOR.* And I am going to leave things as is. I know what I am talking about. No amount of guard can save you thus, humans cannot see the Spiritual Hell they've created here on Earth for self.

Anyone that follows the Abrahamic Law and Laws of Death – Sacrifice, have and has forfeited their life here on Earth.

This a lot of people truly do not know.

IT MATTERS NOT WHICH LODGE OR SORORITY YOU BELONG TO. FROM YOU MAKE A PLEDGE UNTO DEATH, THAT PLEDGE IS FOR LIFE.

YOU ARE BOUND TO DEATH HERE ON EARTH AS WELL AS, IN THE SPIRITUAL REALM. ABSOLUTELY NO ONE CAN GET OUT OF THIS BOND. YOU HAVE NO SOUL. THEREFORE, YOU CANNOT BE SAVED.

YOU HANDED YOURSELF OVER TO DEATH HERE ON EARTH.

Blacks found out in the days of old when it was too late.

A lot of things we say is of God, but none has bothered to question; *WHICH GOD?*

Death is a God. Thus, Hell is the domain of Death.

God did not create Hell. Humans created their own hell with the things they do, what they believe in, and more.

So yes, **HELL IS FULL OF BLACK PEOPLE AND STILL RECRUITING MORE LITERALLY.**

Thus, many have their name being added to the Book of Death literally right now.

Michelle

After writing my above dreams, I went to walk my dog. Did not walk her in that way as I met up with someone I know that lives in the building I live in.

He's on pins and needles. He said, his brother is not doing so well because their mom was diagnosed with Brain Tumor, and the doctors are giving her 1 – 2 months to live.

He also said he has to stay vigil for his brother because he was that close with their mother, and in his state, he's afraid he might jump off the balcony.

I know this is sad for them because years ago I did dream see the death of his (their) mother *but could not tell them.* I so do not know about White People and Spirituality when it comes to dreams.

Plus, it's hard to tell someone you see the death of their parent.

Further, I cannot associate the Diana Ross, Anita Baker dream to what he told me. They are truly different because, like I said, I did see the death of his mother years ago and could not tell him.

Unless it's family, I would rather put what I see in books. Some of my family members have eyes to see so I worry not about family things in that way. What I don't see family wise, others in my family will see, and they will call me and tell me. Some dreams come to pass quickly even before I finish writing a book. Some take months, even years to come to pass.

Like I said; my grandmother had the gift of sight, but her sight is truly different from mine. She could write the Language of God. Therefore, she could pull evil from those who were afflicted with evil. Plus, she could see the dead, and speak to the dead.

I see the dead different, can speak to death thus, my dream world. I speak to the dead, and death this way. Trust me, I truly do not want to see the dead face to face; those at times I see them passing by, can feel them, and more.

After that, the one that I know telling me about his mother and coming back to my apartment with my dog. While making breakfast, *I had this powerful urge,* and right now, I truly do not want to get in the spirit that; **I should tell PEOPLE TO MAKE AMENDS FOR THEIR SINS.**

IF YOU HAVE WRONGED ANYONE IN LIFE, TRULY SEEK FORGIVENESS FOR YOUR WRONGS BECAUSE DEATH IS GOING TO TRULY WALK ON LAND.

DEATH IS COMING BRUTAL TO EARTH.

SO PLEASE, SEEK FORGIVENESS FOR THOSE YOU HAVE WRONGED.
I know some of you believe that your Priest can forgive you of sins but, *NO PRIEST OR PASTOR CAN FORGIVE YOU OF YOUR SINS.*

DOING HAIL MARY'S CANNOT FORGIVE YOU OF YOUR SINS.

Listen, in order for your sins to be taken off your Sin Record, you must ask the person you wronged to forgive you. If that person forgives you then that Sin is taken off your Sin Record, and the Time and Date of forgiveness is recorded.

And no, the person you've wronged do not have to forgive you. And if they do forgive you, they; the person you wronged can ask you for a Sin Offering.

Once you are forgiven of that Sin, you cannot face your Hell for that Sin.

Further know:

NOT ALL SINS ARE/IS FORGIVEN.

SINS DONE AGAINST GOD, ONLY GOD CAN FORGIVE. And God do not have to forgive you because Disobeying God is Automatic Death in Hell – the hell you created for self in Hell if you have divorced God. And many people has and have divorced God literally.

And I am going to stop here because humans truly do not know the truth for real nor do you know what constitutes Physical, and Spiritual Slavery.

Michelle

It's one of those morning where I so do not know where to begin. It seems as if I cannot finish this book.

It's January 28, 2021, and my night was not good. Doing little things to try and help my health but it seems that it's not working.

Blood Pressure shot to hell right now. Hopefully, as the day progress, I will be able to get it under control amongst other things.

A bit down and my energy is off. I now have to wonder, why did I go to sleep?

TAXES DARK BLUE WATER DREAM

Dreamt extremely Dark Blue Rough Water not too long ago. The dream had to do with Taxes; the filing of Income Tax Returns here in Canada. In the dream, I was telling my second child not to go into the water. The water was rough; high, and deep. But as usual my second child did not listen. He went into the Dark Blue Rough Water and began to swim. He did not get too far into the water. He got stuck in the water by a rock beside this man; White Man on the right side of me. On the left side of me, this lady and man also went into the Dark Blue Rough Water and began to swim.

So yes, many are going to either be further bankrupt, and some are going to have to pay back the government come tax time a ridiculous amount of money if they were collecting the government supplement CERB.

Come tax time it is going to be a nightmare for some for real, and I am going to leave it at that because my other dream is a nightmare in my book. This is the second time I am dreaming about war.

JOE BIDEN – AMERICAN WAR DREAM

Book One I talked about the war. The dream I had in Book One had to do with America bullying another nation for power. Thus, I am going to repeat. One demon is gone, and now a worse demon was elected to office. So yes, Death's Book must be fulfilled. Satan did transfer power to Black Death; a Black American. And I will not get into this because DEATH NEED BLOOD.

War must come down to Earth, and war is going to happen. So, while all eyes are on something else – COVID – 19 pandemic, those who run the world behind closed doors have and has set the framework for war to take shape here on Earth.

THE DEVIL'S BOOK MUST BE FULFILLED.

So yes, for the second time in one month I am dreaming America – THE UNITED STATES OF AMERICA going war. I saw the bullets behind this man – the new president of the United States – Biden. He was standing there giving a speech, but I did not see his lips moving. All I saw was bullets being reigned down from the sky and other nations were behind him for starting War.

In the dream I said, *"the citizens are to be blamed for this."* Further, in the dream, I was talking to this gentleman who would remind me of Denzel Washington but was not Denzel Washington *about sin, and the cost of one sin.* There were other Black People in the room that would remind me of Africans – Nigerians.

So, I truly do not know what is going to happen from America to Africa weather wise, and war wise. I am tired of talking – writing. In the dream, I had to defend myself in that; I told them – all Black People that some things I did see and write about but those who I've sent my books too just ignore me. *This is because Blacks did not believe I saw things – what was to come.*

I cannot defend myself. I will not defend myself in real life. What I see is what I see therefore I tell you in these books. Plus, belief is not knowledge. So, if you don't believe me this is good for me. NOW YOU KNOW. YOU HAVE KNOWLEDGE OF WHAT I SEE.

It's up to you to accept me or reject me, and many will reject me. Thus, the one that looked like Denzel Washington stated that; *"Jesus was going to save them from their sins, and I told him Jesus cannot save anyone from their sins."*

In the dream, I wanted to tell them about REVELATIONS of man's so-called holy bible but did not.

Listen, the White Race it seems must fulfill Revelations. *This is their war and BLACK PEOPLE ARE GOING TO GET CAUGHT UP IN THIS NONSENSE – WAR.*

All can be prevented but like I said; DEATH NEED BLOOD – *You the fool fool that run behind your demonic Politicians must follow along with your idiotic politicians thus, your hell literally.*

Was Death talking to me?

MY TALK JANUARY 2021 – BOOK TWO

Yes, but I so cannot remember what Death was telling me. *Thus, the NAMES OF THOSE THAT IS WRITTEN IN THE BOOK OF DEATH.*

Death did become rich off the souls of humans here on Earth. Everything is done. It's time now for Death to take more and more. The weather is going to play a factor too in the way that humans die.

Oh man, I can't remember if this was what Death was telling me, and showing me weather wise with Earth being destroyed.

I am not going to worry about the Destruction of Earth in that way weather wise because; in the dream, I did tell the one that looked like Denzel Washington that; *"only over 100 million will be save and there is over 7 billion people on the Earth,"* and he was in disbelief.

He said, *"140 million and there are billions of people here on Earth."*

I also asked him; *"if he knew the cost of 1 Sin?"* See as humans, many truly do not know of the penalty associated with one sin as many are looking at Jesus to save them; thus, your Religious Beliefs. Therefore, God do not worry about the People of Religion. Absolutely none, that is affiliated with Religion – Death is of God. None will be saved. So yes, Religion has and have deceived billions by taking you away from Life – God.

And yes, I know many of you are saying, no one knows how many people will be saved. Many of you are saying no one knows the minute or the hour.

And I am telling you, *the Righteous KNOWS.* Only you do not know.

God has and have been maintaining the Righteous long before African's gave rise to Death. Broke away from God for Fool's Gold – Death.

So no, I will not get further into this because, it is not going to be pretty real soon. All that is going to happen here on Earth has and have to do with each individual human. Our Sins. Thus, our Life and Death here on Earth.

As for Black Americans, I am going to dedicate *"STOP THE FIGHTING RIDDIM"* mixed by Banton Man to the lots of you.

War is truly not the answer to Life.

Life is the answer to Life.

War is the answer to Death.

Life should not boil down to Death.

<u>"THE WHITE MAN'S GOD IS TRULY NOT THE BLACK MAN'S GOD."</u>

Therefore, know your place in Life with God. As it is, billions have their name in the Book of Death.

Billions cannot be saved. Only over 100 million can be. Therefore, ensure you are a part of the saved. Meaning, ensure your name is in the Book of Life so that you do not have to face hell.

And yes, I had other dreams that I did not include. One specific dream had to do with Prince Harry. But, I am not bothered by the British Monarchy. All I got to say is, "<u>HELL PATIENTLY AWAITS THE LOTS OF THEM."</u>

Not one know that Death not only protect the Children and People of Life. Death protect God as well because, <u>Death ensures no one that has not Life can enter into the Realm of Life – God.</u>

Therefore, only over 100 million can be saved – will enter the Kingdom and Realm of God literally. <u>Thus, FOR MANY BLACKS IT IS CRYING TIME LITERALLY.</u>

Michelle

BOOKS WRITTEN BY MICHELLE JEAN 2021

1) MY TALK JANUARY 2021 - BOOK ONE